you

an introduction

MICHAEL JENSEN

You: An introduction
© Matthias Media 2008

Matthias Media
(St Matthias Press Ltd ACN 067 558 365)
PO Box 225
Kingsford NSW 2032
Australia
Telephone: (02) 9663 1478; international: +61-2-9663-1478
Facsimile: (02) 9663 3265; international: +61-2-9663-3265
Email: info@matthiasmedia.com.au
Internet: www.matthiasmedia.com.au

Matthias Media (USA)
Telephone: 724 964 8152; international: +1-724-964-8152
Facsimile: 724 964 8166; international: +1-724-964-8166
Email: sales@matthiasmedia.com
Internet: www.matthiasmedia.com

ISBN 978 1 921441 18 9

Cover design and typesetting by Matthias Media.

For Catherine

Contents

what, anxious? me?

As I write this, we have come to that important time of the year again: the *Big Brother* season. The human zoo is open for inspection. The usual bunch of annoying but oddly fascinating wannabes are about to become as familiar to us as the people we live with. We see them from every angle. We watch them play and sleep. We speak of them by their first names and instantly know who they are.

It's got me thinking about human beings. Who are we really? What are we supposed to be like? What—or whose—purpose do we serve?

These are good questions—ones each human person has to answer in one way or another. And You aren't any different. Who are You? It's the question Alice in *Alice in Wonderland* has to answer and finds so hard:

> The Caterpillar and Alice looked at each other for some time in silence: at last the Caterpillar took the hookah out of its mouth, and addressed her in a languid, sleepy voice.
> "Who are *you*?" said the Caterpillar.
> This was not an encouraging opening for a conversation. Alice replied, rather shyly, "I-I hardly know, Sir, just at present—at least I know who I was when I got up this morning, but I think I must have been changed several times since then."

> "What do you mean by that?" said the Caterpillar,
> sternly. "Explain yourself!"
> "I can't explain myself, I'm afraid, Sir," said Alice,
> "because I'm not myself you see."[1]

If you had to explain yourself to a large caterpillar sitting on a mushroom smoking a Turkish hookah pipe, what would you say? I know I'd be confused ...

It isn't as easy as it used to be to answer the question of You. French talking head Michel Foucault remarked in the 1960s that he could foresee a time when "man would be erased, like a face drawn in sand at the edge of the sea".[2] Has that day arrived? Is it now impossible to know who You are?

We used to be able to point to our race, class, gender, occupation or family status for an answer. There were boxes you could fit into and locate your identity in. Now, one of the ways in which we live is in rebellion against the boxes that others try to fit us into. That's fair enough: why should we accept the way other people want to define us? But now that we are left to ourselves to define who we are, we find that it isn't that easy. It is an anxious business, being a human.

There are at least seven points of anxiety for modern human beings that I can think of:

1. On the one hand, we speak of the 'human being' as a biological thing—an organism in an environment, a creature of instinct, a package of genes and DNA, a clever animal. The culmination of evolution. The naked ape.

   But on the other hand, we also feel that human beings possess certain qualities that are unique. Human rights, for example. Dignity. Reason. Freedom. Article One of the 1948 Universal Declaration of Human Rights reads, "All human beings are born free and equal in dignity and rights. They are endowed with reason and conscience and should act towards one another in a spirit of brotherhood."[3] We instinctively value human life above the life of other beings, too. For most of us, if our house was burning down, we would rescue Granny and *then* the cat.

2. On the one hand, we live in a narcissistic age. In other words, we are in love with ourselves as creatures. We idolize/idealize the human image. Has any culture spent more time looking in the mirror? The photograph and various telemedia have allowed unprecedented scrutiny of the human face and body. Our heroes are models and sports stars.

   But, on the other hand, with this narcissism has come a lot of hatred of our bodies. Having a body has never been so difficult. Even (maybe even especially!) celebrities get eating disorders.

3. On the one hand, we are in a time of increasing analysis and 'discovery' of the self. We are self-obsessed. That's why we (well, okay, I!) love those personality tests because you (I) can talk about yourself (myself), and other people can talk about themselves at the same time. It's magic.

   But on the other hand, we live in the age of the disappearing 'I'. We delight in the faceless interface of the internet—the creation of masks—of new characters and roles to play. As Demi Moore's character says in the film *Disclosure*:

   > We offer, through technology, what religion and revolution have promised, but never delivered: freedom from the physical body, freedom from race and gender—from nationality and personality, from place and time ... We can relate to each other as pure consciousness.[4]

And yet, our age is also a time of yearning for physical

connectedness with bodily life—the extreme experience, the pierced nipple, the unique tatt. The body is a canvas on which we paint the self so that we can make it unique—just like everyone else.

4. On the one hand, I want to be me, a free, one-of-a-kind individual—free to create my own human being. We want to be free to be an artist of the self: "I'm free to do what I want, any old time".[5]

   But on the other hand, we are lonely because this freedom costs us the joy of other people. Never have so many people lived alone in all of history. The 2001 Australian census showed that 23% of households contain only one resident. According to the Bureau of Statistics, the proportion of people aged 20-25 living alone has nearly doubled over three decades—to 7.1 per cent in 2001. This is true in other western countries too: "This is part of a wider trend, with the proportion of people living alone increasing in each of the five-year age groups, from 20-25 years to 60-64 years, since 1971", the report says.[6] We are attached to detachment.

5. On the one hand, we live to consume. In fact, we are what we consume. A guy called Walter Truett Anderson says, "Consumption is now inseparable from identity".[7] Our individuality and freedom is most enjoyed in our freedom to choose in the shopping mall (although, you have to admit, the freedom to choose in the shopping mall is not really freedom to choose, now, is it? We are made to believe we are choosing when, in fact, the choice has already been made for us, depending on our demographic). We construct our very identity by choosing brands and products. Coke or Pepsi? Apple or Microsoft? The advertising industry has turned us into market segments in increasingly narrow demographics.

   But on the other hand, in support of consumption, work

now consumes us. It demands more and more of our souls as well as our bodies. Back when I was a kid in the 70s, I remember seeing a TV programme about the future—the 'future' being the year 2000 or so—the future now past. One of the amazing prophecies (along with trips to Mars and computers the size of apartment blocks) was the idea that we would only work 20 hours a week and spend the rest of the time hanging out. We called it 'leisure' back then. How much more wrong could that programme have been! People work far longer hours then they ever did. Labour-saving devices produce ... more labour, funnily enough. We have decided that we love to live to work. What we do may be our favourite answer to the question "Who are you?"

6. On the one hand, freedom is what we want to express our humanity, the authentic me. We see this in sexuality. We want freedom to choose whom we have sex with, and when. Freely available contraception has made this seem like a possibility (well, most of the time).

   But on the other hand, the freedom we want is not the sort of freedom we are prepared to give to others. We don't want the pedophile or the rapist to share this freedom. The media fans a general moral outrage against pedophiles (which I like to think comes from the fact that we don't like the inconsistency we see when our own sexual ethics are exposed). Back in May 1968, there was this student revolution in Paris. One of their slogans was "It is forbidden to forbid", which expressed the ultimate rejection of biblical thought (especially in the sphere of sexual behaviours). However, at the same time, the Revolutionary Pederasty Action Committee, a group of pedophiles, produced a manifesto promoting their cause in line with the new spirit of acceptance and tolerance. Strangely, they didn't win many fans or much tolerance. I don't know why; at least they were being consistent ...

7. On the one hand, we delight in increased choice and rapid change—like pigs in mud. We get bored if things don't revamp or grow. We crave the stimulation of the new.

But on the other hand, when experiencing this rapid change, we feel anxious, confused and out of control. We want to take back control of ourselves. One Australian columnist has written, "Control. That's the holy grail [of the times] simply because so many of us feel that life has raced beyond our control."[8]

What these seven tensions or anxieties begin to show is that it is an anxious time to be a human being. I am not saying that being human was easier way back in some golden age; it's just that these are some of the things that make it an anxious business to work out who You are today. It isn't easy to see clearly what it is You are made to do or be. These are general patterns that you can see played out over whole cultures and nations, but they actually affect each one of us as we search to know who it is we are and what it is we are supposed to do with ourselves. On the whole, I think we are struck by what an amazing thing it is to be a human being—to be alive and to be in possession of a body and a mind capable of all the exhilarating experiences of living. But we are also a confused race, unable to master our own power, unable even to know ourselves, bewildered by our own destructiveness.

A GREAT PLAY

The point of this book is to ask what the Bible has to say about You, and to compare it to some of the current alternative views of You. What I am saying is this: You are a 'You' in relation to other Yous—especially in relation to the one who made You in the first place. I want to show how the Bible provides compelling and convincing ways of explaining how things are. Does the Bible say anything to clear up the confusion about who You are? Well I think so.

The Bible is a very old (and sometimes odd) book. The newest bits of it are more than 1,900 years old. But it has a lot to say about You, and it speaks with a remarkable freshness and clarity into our confusion. Frankly, given how hard it is to know ourselves, we need guidance from somewhere ...

The Bible doesn't come to us as a set of rules, nor is it set out like a New Age self-help book. It tells a tale. We could say it is the script of a great play. Its dramatist is the one who made everything (we use the word 'God' to refer to this person)— including the human beings who are its actors. It is a love story—a true love story. It tells how this God loves people, and though they spurn his love, he goes to extraordinary lengths to win them back.

The climax of the play is the entry of Jesus of Nazareth onto the stage. By anyone's standards, Jesus' life was one of the great human lives—the greatest out of all humans who have ever lived—full of wisdom, compassion and wit. But of course, we always execute our best, and that's what happened to Jesus too: they nailed him. This, says the Bible, is where God was winning us back: Jesus' death marked a great defeat of evil—on a cosmic scale, but on a personal level too.

Yet there is more to the tale. There is more to come. It hasn't ended yet. The Bible claims that Jesus will return to rule the world. In the meantime, you are played into the story as a character. This is your cue: what are you going to do? How are you going to respond?

ABOUT THIS BOOK

Essentially, this book is about You: it's about being a human person. As you'll see, in each of the chapters I explore a part of being human. Now, the list that I have come up with isn't necessarily a complete one, but it does give you an introduction to some of the things about being a human being that we just can't avoid but which we always find so complicated. There isn't a particular order to the chapters (apart from the last three) so feel free to read them in the order of your own choosing. Overall, you will find that the book runs roughly from the beginning of life, through its middle and towards what happens at the end of life, and even after. You'll also see that the last three chapters are meant to come at the end, and that they do make sense in the order that they are in.

There's something else you should know about this book before you read on. At the end of each chapter, you'll find some comments and discussion from various people. Some of these comments agree with me, some add things that I haven't addressed, some ask me to be clearer, and some outright disagree with what I have written. Originally I wrote this book as a blog and invited people to comment—which they did. (I got some spam, too, of course!) Some of the people I know personally; some of them I have never met. Some of them are Australians like me; some of them come from—well, they could come from anywhere in the world. But the comments were often so thought-provoking and stimulating, I thought it would be good to include the best of them here. My hope is that they get you thinking as much as they got me thinking.

what You are not

Let's start with a story. It's the story of a man named Job.
It appears in the Old Testament. Job is a rich man and a
righteous man. He has family (seven sons and three daughters)
and possessions aplenty. He goes around to his sons' houses
in turn, and feasts with them. Sounds like a beautiful life! To
complete the picture, the Bible tells us that Job makes sure he
purifies his children by offering sacrifices on their behalf in
case they have sinned by insulting God unintentionally (Job
1:5).

Only in heaven, at the same time, Satan asks the Lord a question.
It is about Job, and it's a pretty good question: "Does Job fear
God for no reason?" (Job 1:9). Satan continues: "After all, he's
got it all pretty good. It's easy to be pure when everything is
sweet. Are you up for a little game? Why not take away his
possessions and see what he does then?" (my paraphrase).

And so an agreement is struck between God and Satan. Satan
goes out and does his worst: Job loses all his possessions, his
family is killed and his flocks are destroyed. He is struck by
wave after wave of calamity. Job grieves his losses, but does
not turn on God and blame him.

The Lord then gloats to Satan: "Did you notice how Job is
still righteous now, Satan?" So Satan ups the ante: "All that

a man has he will give for his life. But stretch out your hand and touch his bone and his flesh, and he will curse you to your face" (Job 2:4-5). God agrees to let Satan do as he will, so Satan inflicts on Job painful sores from the top of his head to the soles of his feet.

Job goes and sits on the local rubbish tip, and takes a piece of broken pottery to scrape the pus off his weeping sores. Even his poor wife comes and says to him, "Do you still hold fast your integrity? [i.e. what's the point?] Curse God and die" (Job 2:9).

Three friends of Job come out to sit with him and comfort him: Eliphaz the Temanite, Bildad the Shuhite and Zophar the Naamathite. They weep for Job's pain and loss, and tear their clothes and sprinkle dust on their heads. No-one says a word for seven days and seven nights.

But then Job speaks up and curses the day of his birth: "Why was I ever born? It'd be far more relaxing to be dead right now than to have suffered my agony" (Job 3:3-13).

Job's friends are well-meaning but hopeless. I once went to the house of a shocked and grieving family. Their relatives were there saying things like "He's in a better place now", or "God meant this for good", or "It's all for the best, you'll see". It probably made the people saying those things feel better, but it was terrible for me, witnessing people in real pain having to listen to such baloney. Job's friends were a lot like those relatives: well-meaning but hopeless. They offer Job page after page of useless advice and cold comforts—some of it quite impeccable theology and beautiful poetry: "Why don't you just pray about it?" "Bad things don't happen to good people, you know." "Your children must have sinned." And they go on. And on. And on.

It makes you want to vomit.

But it all gets quite heated. Job keeps saying to his friends, "How can you argue with God? Wouldn't he just crush you? Isn't he a cruel and distant God—just, but unmerciful, silent and hard? Isn't human life a miserable thing when doing good doesn't even seem to bring rewards? What have I done anyhow? What did I do to deserve this punishment?" But most of all, it is God's silence that disturbs Job: why won't he say anything?

It's a good point. In the end, the platitudes of Job's friends (and even those of a young guy called Elihu who pops up somewhere in the middle) ring hollow. They cannot answer the question, "Why won't the Lord answer Job?"

I haven't had great suffering in my life. But sometimes I feel like Job. My pleas for some explanation for human life seem to echo off the sky. So much suffering seems pointless and undeserved—random, even. What has God got to say about the chaos and mayhem we have to live in? What does he have to say to the family of the boy I knew who lived all of his 18 years under the shadow of cystic fibrosis but struggled on anyway, winning friends and completing his final high school exams, but dying horribly in the months just after graduating? If there is a mighty being at the helm, what has he/she/it got to say?

The question hangs there in the book of Job for 37 chapters or so until we read the most bizarre words: "Then the LORD answered Job out of the whirlwind" (Job 38:1). The Lord proceeds to give poor miserable Job a thorough grilling by asking him the kind of questions you would never want to see on an exam paper: "Where were you when I laid the foundation of the earth? Tell me, if you have understanding" (Job 38:4). Clearly Job has no idea. God asks,

> "Have you commanded the morning since your days began,
>   and caused the dawn to know its place,

that it might take hold of the skirts of the earth,
    and the wicked be shaken out of it?" (Job 38:12-13)

("Um ...well, not lately", you can almost hear Job thinking.)
And God almost gets cheeky with him: "Tell me, if you know
this ... surely you know, for you were already born! You have
lived so many years (not)!"

All of this teaches us two remarkable things about ourselves
as humans. Firstly, Job is told what you and I should learn:
God is God and you are not. Can you claim to have spun the
globe like a top, or to have moulded Sydney Harbour with
the tips of your fingers? Did you stitch together the kangaroo
on your mum's sewing machine? Where are the creatures
you have made? Where are your valleys and hills? Where are
the stars you placed in the sky? Stop kidding yourself that
you have godlike powers. Stop pretending that you can live
independently of your creator. Stop acting like you are wiser
than he is. We human beings, great and wise and beautiful
though we are, are still creatures—limited in understanding,
weak in muscle and prone to getting it wrong. The Lord is God;
you are not.

Secondly, the Lord is more powerful than we are. He can blot
out Job in a second. But he doesn't. And this is the point: *the
Lord is gentle with Job.* He jokes with Job, and even pokes fun
at him. He talks with him. There is definitely a wink in God's
tone in what he says to Job. We are not God, but we humans
have a creator who is gentle and compassionate. We have a
God who stoops—a God who stoops to talk to us and listen to
us. He does not remain a mystery; he answers us.

The end of Job's story is that he is restored to fortune and
family after he repents of speaking beyond his knowledge
(Job 42). The answers to all of Job's questions to God are not

answers, but more questions. But this time the questions are directed back at humans like you. Could you challenge God to a debate and expect to win?

Byron   I've heard it suggested that the problem with Job's friends was lack of prayer. They seemed to know *about* God, but they didn't really *know* God. An interesting thought ...

Craig   It never occurred to me that God was gentle with Job. I thought he was pretty vigorous.

Michael   Well, he doesn't seem that vigorous in the light of the fact that he didn't need to talk at all. He is actually pretty beautiful and amusing in his speech. It is a chiding more than a stern rebuke.

Actually, this is a good point to introduce the next chapter which is about God's great gift to human beings: life itself.

life

LIFE IN KOLDING

After consulting the local veterinarian in the Danish town
of Kolding, the police decided to act. They removed from
an exhibition a work of art with goldfish as the focal point
because an animal rights group had complained that the fish
were in peril. The creation by artist Marco Evaristti consisted of
goldfish swimming inside regular kitchen-blenders. Exhibition
visitors could switch on a blender, transforming the content
to—well, fish soup. Apparently two goldfish had already
perished.[9]

What is so appalling about this story? Goldfish are not
particularly bright or even cute—unlike, say, dolphins. On
any given day, human beings kill and consume hundreds of
millions of formerly living creatures. Flushing a goldfish down
the toilet may not cause you a flicker of bad conscience. You
may even eat bigger and smarter fish. But there is something
almost blasphemous about the public cruelty of this 'work' of
'art', isn't there: using the destruction of another living being
for entertainment feels like a crime against life itself.

This may not surprise you, but You are alive. But what does
that mean? It's really very difficult to say. Life is one of the
most mysterious things of all. We have never been able to

replicate it with our biotechnology. We can engineer genes and clone sheep, but we have never been able to create that spark. The experiments of Dr Frankenstein are still very much imaginary (and they went really well for him now, didn't they?).

Some futurists imagine a world where Artificial Intelligence (AI) is able to regenerate itself independent of human commands—to become a form of 'life'. Computer viruses that run rampant across the world and cause millions of dollars' worth of damage are the vanguard, they say, of independent AI. (Personally, I always wonder why we couldn't just pull the plug out ...)

And yet, somehow, chance was able to make life out of a few carbon-based cells in a primordial puddle—a life that has been passed on in an unbroken chain from living thing to living thing for millions of years until finally ... Michael Jackson. The real difficulty for an atheist is to explain not how human beings evolved from apes, but how human beings evolved from the rocks—and why.

LOVING LIFE

Usually human beings are desperate to preserve the life they have. Aristotle the great Greek once said, "Men cling to life even at the cost of enduring great misfortune".[10] It's an instinctive perception we all have in us: life is better than not-life. The human survival instinct is remarkable.

The true story recorded in the film *Alive* is a great example.[11] An Argentinian rugby team, the Old Christians Club, was on its way to play the Old Boys in Chile when their plane crashed in the Andes. Out of the 45 who took that journey, only 16 returned. For 72 days, the living, in the grip of a nagging hunger and facing their own mortality, were forced to feed off the bodies of those who had been killed in order to survive. Nando Parrado, who was 22 at the time, a second rower and player number 8, said later that the team spirit is what kept the 16 real-life survivors alive. In one startling interview, I read:

> "If we had been soccer players, we would have died [says Parrado].
>
> "Everybody thinks eating human flesh is the most gruesome and terrible thing you can do, but ... it was only one more thing that we did for us to get out. We had to."
>
> Parrado, who is played in the movie by Ethan Hawke, says eating the flesh did not mean they would survive— "There were others who ate the flesh and died anyway, from the avalanche and the cold"—but it did inspire them all the more to escape certain death on the mountaintop.[12]

Our trouble is, Earth is so rich with abundant life that we forget how rare it is in the cosmos. The scalding hot, freezing cold, or gassy planets of our solar system tell us how precise conditions have to be for life—even very simple life—to begin. In 1997, when scientists claimed to have discovered fossilized bacteria in a Mars rock, even President Clinton held a press conference. (I think he was hoping it would distract the media from his ... *cough* ... other matters.) The possible existence of even these simple creatures was exciting because, all of a sudden, life was not as weird as all that. But since then, other scientists have thrown doubt on the original claims. So once again, we are alone.

In actual fact, we are more skilled at killing than keeping life. For every medical discovery, there is the invention of another savage engine of war. Just after the Second Gulf War, the US government began talking about a nuclear 'bunker-buster' bomb. Reports said the envisaged weapon would be an existing

B-61 or B-83 warhead, modified with a ground-penetrating casing, carrying a 300-kiloton charge (which is equivalent to 300,000 tons of TNT). That is 15 times greater than the bomb that flattened the Japanese city of Hiroshima in the August of 1945! It was estimated that such a warhead, used against an underground target in, say, downtown Baghdad, would cause between 10,000 and 40,000 deaths within 24 hours due to radioactive poisoning. (Well that's just great ...)

We have invented philosophies to justify mass killing. The really sickening thing about the Nazi extermination of the Jews was the way in which technology and bureaucracy were harnessed by psychopathic racial hatred. It was like being put to death by the tax department. In our own times, the extremist Islamic beliefs of the 19 World Trade Centre terrorists justified, in their minds, something which, to most of us, is an outrage which resulted in the deaths of more than 3,000 people on a Monday morning.

We drive cars that fart lethal gases into the atmosphere, we kill animals for sport, we reduce biodiversity by demolishing habitats, we spray with poison life we don't like, we are horrified at the killing of criminals or whales but, at the same time, we're happy for the government to sanction the killing of the unborn (some 73,000 in Australia in 2001). And we say we 'love life'.

HEAVY BREATHING OR THE KISS OF LIFE

So what are we to make of this 'life'? As the Bible has it, life comes from the living God. He breathes the breath of life into all living things, and they depend on him for ongoing life. Have a look at this:

> These are the generations
> of the heavens and the earth when they were created,
> in the day that the LORD God made the earth and the
>   heavens.
>
> When no bush of the field was yet in the land and no
> small plant of the field had yet sprung up—for the LORD
> God had not caused it to rain on the land, and there was
> no man to work the ground, and a mist was going up
> from the land and was watering the whole face of the
> ground—then the LORD God formed the man of dust from
> the ground and breathed into his nostrils the breath of life,
> and the man became a living creature. (Gen 2:4-7)

Humanity was created by God from the dust of the ground
with his "breath of life". Life—your life—just is. Some say that
life is a gift, but the Bible pictures it more as a loan. Life is
God's, not ours. We receive it from God's kiss. This means
we give account only to him at the end for our life. We have
been given the beautiful freedom of life in order that we might
honour the giver of life—the living God. And ever since the
making of the first man and the first woman, God has enlisted
the help of human beings in making life. Making life is part
of their task: they are to "be fruitful and multiply and fill the
earth" (Gen 1:28).

Of course, we don't like the idea of life not being our own.
The interference of parents and teachers and governments and
bosses in our lives is something we resent, and often reject. "I'll
live my life how I want" is our personal national anthem.

Up to a point, we are right: our lives do not belong to another
human being. No human has the power to control your life.
But declaring independence from the source of life is bizarre.
It's a bit like all the vacuum cleaners of the world saying "Life

sucks!" (sorry, that was a bad pun) and uniting in defiance against the dictatorship of the power sockets. Can you explain your life? Can you die and live again? Did you give yourself life that you now own your life?

Thinking this way was humanity's crucial mistake. Originally we had from God a life uncompromised by death. But because we denied the source of life itself—because we, in our arrogance, imagined ourselves givers to ourselves of our own lives—our lives have become something we know only as a fragment of time. Life as we know it is a thing that will one day end. (But more about that later ...)

You share life with the plants and animals, but you are not like them. Human life is a different sort of life. In Genesis 1, we read the famous words about humans being created in the "image of God" (Gen 1:27). It's an amazingly rich phrase, this "image of God", and it means, in part, that human life is very close to God's own life. We catch his glory and project it to the cosmos—something no animal can claim to do.

AN IMAGE PROBLEM?

Across Iraq, the statues of Saddam Hussein stood as powerful reminders of his power over the Iraqi people. Obviously the statues were not Saddam, but when it came time to overthrow the tyrant, the people slapped shoes in his face in an act of defiance as if the statues were really him. We are God's image just like those statues were images of Saddam. (You *do* get that I think Saddam and God are very different, don't you? Please say yes!)

In the Bible's words, we have been given "dominion" over the other things that live (Gen 1:26). We have a responsibility to tend life on our planet—to name it, nurture it and multiply it.

Therefore, we need to respect it. This idea of responsibility for life was something that the boys in my Year 8 class recognized immediately as part of being human without referring to Genesis at all. Our life is obviously very different from that of our pets: we have the capacity for empathy, imagination and creativity, and self-reflection, whereas they do not. We name things. We can imagine not being. Does a dog contemplate its death? (Well, the ones I interviewed for this book didn't ...)

Life is always good—in fact, it is very good. We know it and feel it to be true. Life is delicious. In Hebrew, they used the word '*tov*', which means 'beautiful' and 'enjoyable' as well as 'morally good'. The verdict of the Lord on the sixth day of creation (which was when he created an abundance of life) was to call what he had made "very *tov*" (Gen 1:31).

So we have been given the responsibility for life, we might say. God has created in us the capacity for speaking—for passing on communication from him and to him, and from and to other forms of life. To us has been given the role of tending and caring for other types of life. This is a job we are well-equipped to do. The dolphins may be smarter, but not having opposable thumbs is a significant limitation. And no-one thinks of dolphins as being responsible, now, do they?

WHAT'S SO GOOD ABOUT IT?

But why is human life good? Human life is good because it is a trace of the glory of God himself. Humankind has been made by God "a little lower than the heavenly beings" and "crowned ... with glory and honour" (Ps 8:5). In Psalm 8, the whole point is that the specialness of human life to God is a matter of wonder: it's weird that he would make us so important. It's weird but it's true.

Saying that life is good is not saying that it is the *only* good, or that it is the *absolute* good. Sometimes when we talk about life being 'sacred', we don't really capture the Bible's vision of life because there are some things that are not worth living for. There are some occasions when to choose to lay down your life for your friends is actually the better way.

So what is the best way to live this life—this opportunity of a space of time to be alive? It is distressing to think that most of us use our lives merely to accumulate stuff, to revel in pleasure or to make an indentation in a couch while watching junk on TV. What we want is a way of forgetting that time—and therefore life—is running out. We are alive, but we are not experts at living. Some of us just *exist* instead of live. The wisdom writers of the Bible label this kind of non-life 'foolishness' ...

9 COMMENTS

Drew   Apparently kids flushed goldfish down the toilet after watching *Finding Nemo* in order to set them free.

              What's the link between life and freedom?

Michael   Well, I think life and freedom are bound together: the gift of life is a gift of a kind of freedom. But this freedom is a 'creaturely freedom'—the freedom to be human, not the freedom to master life. The fact that life comes to us from elsewhere—from outside ourselves—and that we are powerless to stop it slipping away ought to remind us that our freedom has sharp limits. We'll have a look at freedom later.

           I think the work of art—the fish in the blender—actually asks a question of us: do we think life itself, in whatever form, is somehow sacred? The trouble is, how do we make sense of this 'sacred' idea? Where does it come from? In that sense, it is really successful art—even if it is kinda sick.

Byron   We love life, but then we buy McDonalds ...

Michael   Well, food is kind of an interesting sign of our pleasure in life, isn't it? Eating well is a celebration of the goodness of life. But, like so many things, we can't have it without having it in excess.

Byron   ▶ *"Up to a point, we are right: our lives do not belong to another human being. No human has the power to control your life."*

Wait a minute: our lives *do* belong to other people. Who we are—the moral decisions we make—are not taken in an individualistic vacuum; they come from within communities that shape who we are and to whom we are indebted. I am not free to reject God as the source of life and live my own little project. And it is also true that I am not free to reject all cultural influences and live my own little culture-less life. We have real commitments (some explicit, some implicit) to other people; other people can and should tell us what to do—and we should listen.

Of course, that said, the communities we live in have a responsibility to assess critically the commitments they demand of us. For example, they have to decide how long car drivers stay on their provisional license under its rules before they can graduate to their full license. What's more, they also have a responsibility to free us from false commitments, such as the requirement that we only marry someone from a particular ethnic group.

Drew   See, I think the key word here is 'responsibility'. No-one likes hearing about responsibilities. It's what our mum lectures us on.

But perhaps there is a type of responsibility that, instead of feeling like a ball and chain, actually gives us freedom?

Michael   Oh, *Mum!*

Well, I think so. We keep losing the 'response' part of the word 'responsibility': in taking responsibility, we are answering to and for the freedom we have been given in life.

Benjamin ▶ *"We are God's image just like those statues were images of Saddam."*

In the 'we', do you include Saddam?

Why does (your) God create/allow such poor images of himself? Saddam certainly wouldn't have allowed it.

Michael   Yes, Saddam is included. That's the scary thing, actually: we can't dehumanize someone like Saddam, no matter what he does ...

To answer your question (or to at least try), when Saddam made statues, they were almost always bigger than him. The image was used to make him look bigger and more powerful than he is. God couldn't do this; what could be bigger than him? So his images are all smaller—lesser—than he. Saddam's way isn't how God works; God tends (as the Bible tells us) to show his power in gentleness, rather than in brute force.

touched

TOUCH ME

A lot of people characterize the Bible as being opposed to the human body. But, as the great Christian writer CS Lewis once said:

> Christianity is almost the only one of the great religions which thoroughly approves of the body–which believes that matter is good, that God Himself once took on a human body, that some kind of body is going to be given to us even in Heaven and is going to be an essential part of our happiness, our beauty and our energy.[13]

However, it seems to me that, of all the issues we face in contemporary life, none confuses us more than the human body. We are at the same time fascinated and repelled–obsessed and repulsed–delighted and revolted–by our bodies. Human life is but a wrestle with the body. We admire both indulgence and restraint. We want pleasure, but we also want to look good.

Our visual-oriented world is filled with images of ideal bodies–bodies which *appear* real (because photography and film are 'realistic media'), but bodies which are, at best, semi-real–bodies which have been airbrushed, cropped and re-coloured. We are now being confronted with a glut of fake plastic bodily beauty. There are no bad hair days, no cellulite, no love handles and no muffin tops.[14] In this world of images, beauty is normal—boring, even.

A small handful of men and women are held up as having the perfect bodies—supermodels, sportsmen, actors and so on. The rest of us inhabit a different plane where bodily beauty is rare. Occasionally we receive a visit from the realm of perfection, but since, in reality, these men and women are as mortal as we are, they prefer to keep a safe distance.

The flip side (or is it a contradiction?) of this is that advances in technology now allow us to detach the self from the body. Online, I can be a pure self with no body—I can be in two places at once: on the internet *and* in my room—whereas, previously, my presence was limited to my physical whereabouts. Communication technology has given us the impression that we can go beyond the limits and defects of the body. We have become like gods. Or so we think.

Is the body a machine—a predictable system? Is it a case for the soul—a jar for our identities? Or is it all of me? Is it a canvas that I can pierce, paint and prick in order to display my identity to the world?

It seems to me that owning a body is a confusing thing for a lot of people. In discussing drugs, alcohol or sexuality, for example, students I have spoken to claim that they—and only they—have power over their own bodies. However, they also admit they lack control over them. The senses of our bodies give us tremendous pleasure, but so often we abuse our bodies in seeking pleasure.

A TOUCHING STORY

Here's a touching story, from Mark's Gospel:

> ... when Jesus had crossed again in the boat to the other
> side, a great crowd gathered about him, and he was beside
> the sea. Then came one of the rulers of the synagogue,
> Jairus by name, and seeing him, he fell at his feet and
> implored him earnestly, saying, "My little daughter is at
> the point of death. Come and lay your hands on her, so
> that she may be made well and live." And he went with
> him.
>
> And a great crowd followed him and thronged about
> him. And there was a woman who had had a discharge of
> blood for twelve years, and who had suffered much under
> many physicians, and had spent all that she had, and was
> no better but rather grew worse. She had heard the reports
> about Jesus and came up behind him in the crowd and
> touched his garment. For she said, "If I touch even his
> garments, I will be made well." And immediately the flow
> of blood dried up, and she felt in her body that she was
> healed of her disease. And Jesus, perceiving in himself that
> power had gone out from him, immediately turned about
> in the crowd and said, "Who touched my garments?" And
> his disciples said to him, "You see the crowd pressing
> around you, and yet you say, 'Who touched me?'" And
> he looked around to see who had done it. But the woman,
> knowing what had happened to her, came in fear and
> trembling and fell down before him and told him the
> whole truth. And he said to her, "Daughter, your faith
> has made you well; go in peace, and be healed of your
> disease." (Mark 5:21-34)

My mum went to visit some Christians working in a fistula hospital in Ethiopia. What's a fistula? Well, technically, it is a perforation between the bladder and vagina, or the rectum and the vagina, which causes urinary or fecal incontinence. The perforation often occurs during difficult childbirth. I wouldn't be so graphic about it if it wasn't such a real problem.

Many of the girls—some of them barely teenagers—who have found their way to the hospital had to struggle through childbirth in distant villages where there is no medical assistance. As a result, they were left with no bladder and/or bowel control. The constant flow of urine and feces makes them undesirable to their husbands, and because of their smell, they are usually left alone in huts on the fringes of their villages.

It is hard for us hygienic and healthy westerners to imagine the self-loathing, despair and unspeakable isolation that these women face. But the woman in this story from Mark's Gospel knew. She only touched Jesus' cloak, but this in itself was a desperate act from a desperate woman—a person who felt acute shame for her troublesome body which had not been healthy or holy (because it was unhealthy) for 12 years. Whatever her condition (and most commentators speak of it as some kind of gynaecological haemorrhage), it must have filled her with self-disgust. It must have isolated her from family and community life, both practically and spiritually. Jesus uses the word *'mastigos'* to refer to her suffering (v. 34): it means torment or affliction, and it's used to describe the sort of ritual floggings that were dished out by the religious authorities—something that Jesus would experience in his own body soon enough. This poor woman suffered from *mastigos*. For 12 years.

THE OOZE

Uncleanness was a human problem. It was not just a female problem or a male problem; it was a human problem. The Old Testament talks about this woman's condition (along with other oozings of the male and female body) in the book of Leviticus:

> "If a woman has a discharge of blood for many days, not at the time of her menstrual impurity, or if she has a discharge beyond the time of her impurity, all the days of the discharge she shall continue in uncleanness. As in the days of her impurity, she shall be unclean. Every bed on which she lies, all the days of her discharge, shall be to her as the bed of her impurity. And everything on which she sits shall be unclean, as in the uncleanness of her menstrual impurity. And whoever touches these things shall be unclean, and shall wash his clothes and bathe himself in water and be unclean until the evening. But if she is cleansed of her discharge, she shall count for herself seven days, and after that she shall be clean. And on the eighth day she shall take two turtledoves or two pigeons and bring them to the priest, to the entrance of the tent of meeting. And the priest shall use one for a sin offering and the other for a burnt offering. And the priest shall make atonement for her before the LORD for her unclean discharge." (Lev 15:25-30)

Why was there such a concern for bodily hygiene among God's people? Was it because they had hang-ups about it? The Bible gives us a clue a little later on: "Thus you shall keep the people of Israel separate from their uncleanness, lest they die in their uncleanness by defiling my tabernacle that is in their midst" (Lev 15:31). The purity of the individual body was necessary for maintaining the purity of everybody. The system of holiness—the classification of things as clean, unclean or holy—was a powerful symbol of the 'not-goodness' of sinful humanity. It was a symbol of the human need for holiness which couldn't come naturally: it needed to come from God. It was built into the daily routines of the people as they tended and cared for their own bodies. It was an external symbol of an inner condition. It was a reminder of the limits and fragility of the body, cursed since the Garden of Eden where, although they had been made in God's image (for he had intended men and women to represent him bodily), the man and the woman had covered themselves out of shame (Gen 3).

God, of course, has no such bodily inconveniences. In the ninth century BC, the prophet Elijah teased the priests of Baal about their god by saying, "Perhaps Baal is on the loo, or having an afternoon nap because he's tired!" (my paraphrase of 1 Kings 18:27). A real god wouldn't have to do those things!

However, as the Creator of life, things marked with the stain of death had to be excluded from God's presence. Blood was a symbol of life. That was why Israelites did not eat blood in their meat. The blood of animal sacrifices made atonement for their sins and was sprinkled on them to make them pure. But loss of blood (suggesting loss of life) caused uncleanness.

DEAD WOMAN WALKING

Like some weird game of tip, the state of uncleanness was contagious through touch. The unclean man or woman had to regard the things they touched as unclean, too—especially beds and clothes. Being unclean meant that, temporarily, you had no place in community with others or with God. Atonement was needed to restore you.

The concept of uncleanness did not reflect a particular kind of sinfulness in the person. Having a period or a discharge or a skin disease wasn't a sin. Such things did not mean that the body was, by nature, evil; rather, it signified that the body lived in the realm of sin and was under the sentence of death. To this woman from Mark's story and her community, then, this woman reeked of death. She was a non-person—a walking semi-corpse.

Pagan readers would also have recognized this woman's situation. Ancient physicians, completely flummoxed by the female body, considered every illness of a woman the result of a drying up of the womb because of lack of sex. That was their best theory! Archaeologists have discovered that women in the Roman Empire used to wear little charms to protect them from such a fate, looking to a divine solution to the earthliness of their bodies.

And so, out of her desperation, this woman is led to a shocking crossing of boundaries. She had suffered for years under the expensive bogus medicine prescribed by all the local quacks, but instead of improving, her condition had worsened under their treatments (Mark 5:26). It was just a touch that she wanted—wanted almost superstitiously—and yet it was touch, the contact of the clean with the unclean, that was the problem. But immediately her bleeding dried up and she felt released from her suffering (Mark 5:29).

GO IN PEACE

Jesus caused a short circuit in the system of holiness. Contact with his body did not infect him; instead, the opposite was true. The presence of his body brought life, not death. His touch even revived the dead girl in Mark 5:41-42. When Paul says Jesus came "in the likeness of sinful flesh" (Rom 8:3), he didn't mean that Jesus had a fake body; rather, Jesus' holiness wasn't compromised by the indignities of having a physical nature, or by walking among and even touching those who possessed this sort of decaying mortal body. In addition, Jesus fulfils the requirements of the law—even these weird bits from Leviticus 15—by having a holy body and, ultimately, defeating sin in his body and triumphing over death. By his bleeding, oozing wounds we are healed (Isa 53:5).

Therefore, we no longer need a symbol of our distance from God. What we need now is a reminder of God's nearness to us. The barrier is there, but the barrier has been crossed. God's character as the giver of life, wholeness and normality, which was so graphically illustrated in the old law, has not been abolished, but rather now it has been demonstrated dynamically in the flesh—in what Jesus did. The deathly stench of our bodies does not impede our progress into the presence of God to sit at his table. All the fear, shame and self-loathing that the woman felt disappeared. Jesus told her to "go in peace"—in *shalom*. (*'Shalom'* is a Hebrew word meaning 'wholeness, completion, fulfilment, fellowship with others'.)

I remember going to the Paralympics in Sydney. It was extremely confronting to spend a day watching amputees, blind people and people in wheelchairs. I am ashamed to say I found it very difficult. It's no wonder that people in our world experience the same kind of isolation that this woman did, along with its deadening spiritual effects. Uncleanness is not just an Ethiopian problem; our own community has its untouchables—that is, those who are the living dead: the disabled, the severely ill, the chronically ill, the addicted, the obese, the elderly and so on. The weakness of the body excludes them from full citizenship. We prefer not to look at such bodies, let alone touch them.

And yet the touch of Jesus makes everything different.

Byron
So often I took my body for granted, only noticing when there was pain or something wrong. It was a tool to be used. Health faded into the background as a general blessing for which I was occasionally and sporadically thankful.

Having cancer recently has made me realize again what a gift life is. Each breath comes to us undeserved and free. There is a limit, but with such an abundance, my body, even when it's not working 100%, has become a new-found reason for thankfulness. Bodies enable so much of what it is to be human—to smile, to embrace, to be vulnerable, to be both unavoidably interwoven with the world and yet a thing, separate and individual.

Bodies are wonderful. I'm a fan.

Michael
Yes, I like having a body! One of the things I have realized lately is how much a part of your body your brain is. You can't think or write if you are tired or hungry. You do have to be in the mood, and you have to make sure your body is looked after if you are to think well. Weird huh? I guess I shouldn't be so surprised, but my default position was that somehow the two were separate.

Byron
It works the other way too: your mental attitudes can affect your level of energy and general health. Stress can cause all kinds of physical effects.

Rhea
The woman's gutsy-ness is pretty cool. I often feel embarrassed about expressing how much I need God ('cause I am meant to be a 'together' sort of person!). Even though I know God's response, I fear other people's. It stops me from relating to God and receiving from him sometimes. Humility can be hard ...

Michael
Yes, she is brave/scared. Her touch is a great image of faith, though, isn't it? Yes, it is courageous. It is risky, even. But is it

also a nothing—a simple, unsophisticated, humble reaching out, nothing more?

Byron   A god who needs to go to the toilet and to bed: I've heard these taunts from Elijah used to mock the idea that Jesus might be divine.

Michael   Yes, that's ironic, isn't it? That would be an Islamic point of view, I guess. And it is right—up to a point: the infinite God does not suffer the indignities and limitations of a human body. Or at least, he doesn't have to ...

Joanna   Wow, that last paragraph is extremely powerful ... Sometimes those demarcations of difference are so clear to me in my daily life, it is wonderful to consider that Jesus crosses those boundaries.

But I was wondering if you could explain a little more about how Jesus had a holy body. Did he obey the law in full, with all the washing and cleansing and everything? Or was his body just inherently holy?

Michael   That's made me think and go back to the Gospels. We do hear that Jesus was circumcised, for example, which was the way in which bodies were designated as belonging to God's people. When we see him encountering unclean people like lepers or the dead, we don't hear that he went and had a wash afterwards. His holiness in his body had made them clean, of course. Mark tells us that he declared all foods clean—that the old food laws (not eating pork, etc.) no longer held (Mark 7:19). Got any thoughts?

Joanna   Jesus, being God, was holy anyway, and therefore didn't need to be made holy by washing, remaining isolated or making sacrifices (and seeing as that was the point of those things, I think Jesus didn't need to do them). Those things signified holiness rather than bringing it about in themselves, right?

Michael   Well, yes Joanna, I think that's right. Getting baptized and
           having the Holy Spirit had a lot to do with it, though. It
           showed that he was pure.

body

TATTOO YOU

Does it matter what you do with your body? Can't you do what you want with—and to—your body? Whose body is it, anyway?

Perhaps the most visible sign in our culture of people being anxious about the body is the emergence of body piercing as a widespread practice since the early to mid-1990s. Once a sign of primitive culture, body piercing has now been taken up by many wealthy and technologically sophisticated young westerners (including a few related to me!). What was once only seen on the pages of *National Geographic* now walks the streets of the inner city.

But what does it mean? Is it just a fad—like your dad's sideburns in the 70s, or your big brother's pink shirts in the 80s? (I was one of those big brothers ... I even had pointy grey shoes ...) Or has it got a deeper significance than that? Sociologists certainly think so. Marking the body in this way—or in any way (e.g. haircuts)—has to do with how you see yourself in relation to other bodies. It places you in a conversation with your society.

In our culture, body piercing is a declaration of independence in defiance of 'normality', and even in defiance of nature.

Social commentator Anthony Giddens argues that, at the beginning of the 21st century, as people lose faith in religion, family duties and hard work as ways of making life meaningful, they are instead attempting to construct the self upon all that seems to remain solid and tangible: their physical bodies.[15] Some say that body piercing is an attempt to write the meaning of the body over and against its biology: the body and the self are raw materials that you, the artist, get to shape—the blank piece of paper on which you can write the story of your life. For postmodern thinkers, the human body is not only a building site of the identity, it is also the site of a power struggle. Whose idea of the body will win? Who will get to determine the body's meaning? Who will say what a body will be like—in its maleness or femaleness, for example? Will the geneticist map out the shape of my life in her codes, predicting my addictions? Piercing is a dramatic statement of ownership of one's own skin in defiance of those who would control it. It says, "I am not the victim".

TATTOO YOU TWO

I found evidence for this view in some interviews with piercing afficionados. Bill, for example, says that his piercing is to do with "the mapping of his own history and personal evolution". His piercings and tattoos have a "synergistic effect on his life", making an "alternative spirituality" possible. Louise, who runs a body piercing business in Melbourne, says that people are "reclaiming their bodies". She thinks many of her clients are "on the search, searching for meaning, and for feelings of belonging to something larger than themselves that isn't religious". Another woman said, "I really like the way my body looks a lot better now. I have been a heavy person all my life and my body felt out of my control. Body modification is totally within my control."[16]

Piercing the body is real. In contrast, so much of contemporary life is virtual. Piercing is something that you and you alone can do. It is authentic. It is an expression of autonomy—of freedom—from parents, uniforms, social pressure and even biology.

Now there's a question: is the body biologically fixed? Or is it a piece of mouldable clay with a story yet to be told? How does the body fit in relation to other bodies in society?

The Bible's testimony is that the body is made and has a maker. The body has an author who intends it for the work of naming, taming and filling the earth. From their bodies, humans are to bring forth other bodies.

The poet of Psalm 139 knew what it means to be a made body:

> For you formed my inward parts;
>   you knitted me together in my mother's womb.
> I praise you, for I am fearfully and wonderfully made.
> Wonderful are your works;
>   my soul knows it very well.
> My frame was not hidden from you,
> when I was being made in secret,
>   intricately woven in the depths of the earth.
> Your eyes saw my unformed substance;
> in your book were written, every one of them,
>   the days that were formed for me,
>   when as yet there was none of them. (Ps 139:13-16)

The body is intimately known and wonderfully shaped by its creator. It has been 'knitted together' in ways even we with our medical science do not yet understand. Having a body formed in the darkness before we were conscious, taken from the one sperm in a hundred million that got through to the ovum which then grew to pulse with life and thoughts, should make us all the more aware of our utter dependence on our Creator. Were you there when your body was formed? Did you select the sperm? Did you form your hands, your eyes, your nerves or your brain? Do you know about your genetic code? Do you know the number of your days, or the number of hairs on your head?

PINOCCHIO, PERHAPS?

Seen in this light, the human claim of having absolute rights over our bodies is highly questionable. Our declaration of independence from God as bodies is not only wrong, it is silly. Isaiah says:

> "Woe to him who strives with him who formed him,
>   a pot among earthen pots!
> Does the clay say to him who forms it, 'What are you
>   making?'
>   or 'Your work has no handles'?
> Woe to him who says to a father, 'What are you
>   begetting?'
>   or to a woman, 'With what are you in labor?'"
>   (Isa 45:9-10)

There are no rebellious little Pinocchios in this scene ...

Our true human identity is not something we create or construct, but something we receive and realize. Our bodies, like our lives, are on loan. The things we do that damage our bodies are not merely wrong, they are not what we were made for. They are unnatural.

I am not saying that your body belongs to another human being from whom you've borrowed it; I am saying that it belongs to a holy God whose character is merciful and gracious, slow to anger and abounding in love.

Isaiah was talking not just about humanity; he was talking about God's own people, the Israelites. The Israelites were created from a nation of enslaved bodies. The people of Israel pierced their bodies as a sign that they belonged to God. Circumcision was a mark in the flesh signifying that they and their children belonged to God. They were the children of Abraham according to the flesh.

NOT YOUR OWN

Those who understand themselves as having been remade as human beings because of Jesus Christ must understand the preciousness of their bodies. They have a kind of spiritual biology—but not in the sense that their bodies are now unimportant. It's quite the opposite, in fact. Have a look at what Paul says:

> "All things are lawful for me," but not all things are helpful. "All things are lawful for me," but I will not be enslaved by anything. "Food is meant for the stomach and the stomach for food"—and God will destroy both one and the other. The body is not meant for sexual immorality, but for the Lord, and the Lord for the body. And God raised the Lord and will also raise us up by his power. Do you not know that your bodies are members of Christ? Shall I then take the members of Christ and make them members of a prostitute? Never! Or do you not know that he who is joined to a prostitute becomes one body with her? For, as it is written, "The two will become one flesh." But he who is joined to the Lord becomes one spirit with him. Flee from sexual immorality. Every other sin a person commits is outside the body, but the sexually immoral person sins against his own body. Or do you not know

that your body is a temple of the Holy Spirit within you,
whom you have from God? You are not your own, for you
were bought with a price. So glorify God in your body.
(1 Cor 6:12-20)

The Christian—doubly so—does not belong to himself or herself.
The Corinthians were famous for their love of pleasure and
passion. Yet, against the Corinthian culture of indulgence of
the body, Paul argues that the re-created body of the Christian
has a different purpose: the body is now "for the Lord"—the
Lord Jesus, in other words. The redeemed body is not intended
for *porneia*—that is, sexual immorality (yeah, that's the word
we get 'pornography' from), but for doing the deeds of Christ.
Our bodies are parts of *his* body.

BODY PIERCING SAVED MY LIFE

Part of the brilliance of what Paul does in this passage from 1
Corinthians is that he lets the various meanings of the word
'body' overlap: the human body, the church 'body' and the
body of Jesus Christ. An action in one body affects the other
two. Sleep with a prostitute and you are sinning against the
body. Which body? All three. This is why what you do with
your body as a member of Christ's body matters—if you belong
to him, that is.

To you, Paul's teaching that "You are not your own" (v. 19)
might be repulsive, sounding much like a justification for the
use of one body by another. Victims of child sexual abuse may
feel as if their bodies have been stolen from them by another.
(That the abusers of the bodies of children and young people
have been allowed to carry on in churches with the merest slap
on the wrist is appalling—not just because of the evil itself,
but because we church people have failed in our responsibility

to keep the body of Christ pure.) To the feminist movement, the use and abuse of the individual female body by society is blamed, at least in part, on church attitudes. The argument in favour of abortion rights is, in fact, an argument about rights over bodies. And Christian opposition to abortion is seen as an attempt to subdue and control the bodies of women further.

But there is a difference: Jesus Christ has not stolen our bodies, or bullied his way into power over them. He has bought them—bought them at the cost of his own body. He does not make us his victims in order to subdue and control our bodies. Instead, he becomes the victim: he voluntarily submits his body to be victimized—to be pierced, nails driven through his hands and feet, and a spear into his side—in order to purchase freedom for our bodies, releasing us from the control of evil.

Submitting your body to this Lord's ownership is not offering it to be abused or dominated, but allowing it to achieve the glory and honour for which it was made—a body united to other bodies in the body of Christ.

SLIM FOR HIM?

What does it look like, then, to "glorify God in your body" (1 Cor 6:20)? Is it okay to engage in body piercing or to smoke? Is it honouring to God to be overweight, or should we be 'Slim for Him'[17] and 'firm believers'? What about tattoos and plastic surgery?

These questions kind of miss the point. Honouring God with your body, as Paul describes it, has to do with seeing your body as a member with other bodies of the body of Christ. Does what you do with your body build up Christ's body, or does it threaten to tear it down? This is the crucial question we need to ask ourselves before going on to think about those other questions I just raised. On the whole, Christians seek to act in harmony with the body of Christ—not suppressing their individuality so that everyone dresses, acts and talks the same, but not defying the community into which they and their bodies have been built.

The way God wants us to live is not *without* a body, but *with* our bodies. The body is profoundly precious for it has been made *and* redeemed. So what we do with our flesh really counts.

8 COMMENTS

Byron	*"Piercing is a dramatic statement of ownership of one's own skin in defiance of those who would control it."* Ironically, piercing (and/or tattoos) can also mean the opposite: it can signify the marking of a slave, a concubine, a prisoner—that is, an owned body (cf. branding of animals).
Julia	Too right, Byron. Until recently, the tattoo was only seen on the seaman or bikie: the social outcasts and misfits.
Byron	Is body piercing/tattooing actually damaging? What about getting a haircut or clipping your toenails? Is the difference that the former are more permanent? (Though piercings can be 'undone' by letting them heal, and tattoos can, with difficulty, be erased, I think.) What about over/undereating? Is this another way we try to claim our bodies?
Michael	No, body piercing, tattooing and so on aren't necessarily damaging at all (though the jury is still out on male circumcision!). But even getting a haircut is a deliberate alteration of the 'nature' of our bodies.

It isn't damaging but it's definitely not just a matter of looking 'good'. It is a statement of my identity in relation to other identities. It says something, whether I am trying to be the same as them, or whether I'm trying to be different.

Eating is interesting. I suppose drug/alcohol abuse is similar. Nobody, I assume, overeats in order to *look* fat, whereas the opposite is true of undereating ... (I assume; these things are complex).

Sam

1 Corinthians 6 is such a profound text for me as I try to get my head around what God thinks of me. I am reminded that God is not just concerned with the 'spiritual' bits of me. He made me as matter that matters. Therefore, I need not follow a misguided religiousness that says sex is unspiritual (1 Cor 7) —hooray! But before I get too carried away, there's no sexual immorality either.

Could you say something about sex and forgiveness?

Michael

I didn't want to address the issue of sexual sin as if it was the only way to talk about the body. What I am trying to emphasize here is that we don't own our bodies outright, much as we like to think we do. Of course, sexual activity is where we see what people think of their bodies. You do hear people saying "It's just sex", meaning that it doesn't mean anything in particular. We are just pieces of meat—mammals on the Discovery Channel, as the song says.[18] This is probably a reaction to some religious people who have been, perhaps, overly negative about sex. But it isn't just sex because your body is involved: *you* are involved! Saying "It's only sex" is basically admitting that you are something else apart from your body, and giving in to the fantasy that you can cordon off yourself from your body in some way. But we know this isn't true: what happens to your body affects you as you. You said it well: you're "matter that matters".

What about forgiveness, and 'getting out of it'? Well, I think we need to hear that we have been forgiven even for our misuse of our bodies. But this is hard to believe because of the mess we cause—mess which is always there to remind us. We don't just get forgiveness, though; we get holiness too. God doesn't just forgive us, he purifies us in Jesus. He makes us acceptable for inclusion in his family, his holy and pure people.

Can we change? Not humanly. Keeping a pure body isn't possible without divine help—something I know from personal experience. I don't want to offer tips either (e.g. take a cold shower). The only tip Paul offers is "Flee" (1 Cor 6:18)—that is, "Get the Sam Hill out of there!"

Anonymous   Thanks, Michael! What you've written here is a real challenge to the individualistic nature of our society—a challenge not to see ourselves primarily as individuals with bodies, but individuals who are part of the body of Christ.

But if "what we do with our flesh really counts", shouldn't we be concerned with health and weight issues? If my weight impacts my ability to do what God wants me to do, doesn't it matter?

Michael   Well, I am unsure of what the criterion of an "ability to do what God wants me to do" is. It is too performance-oriented. That's not our God. The poet John Milton, as he was going blind, wondered how he could serve God without sight, and penned the line "They also serve who only stand and wait". [19]

I would certainly say that culpable poor health is dishonouring to the creator/redeemer of the body. It does him no glory for a person to misuse their body. Of course, an individual body's ill health affects others around them, too. So, if that's what you mean, then yes, you can mismanage your bodily life so badly that you limit your ability to love the people around you. But this will mean very different things for different people, because our bodies are so, well, *different.*

Looking back over this chapter, I wonder if I have been positive enough about the glorious body. I don't want to be seen as saying that the body is a problem that needs to be overcome! That's not what I am trying to say at all. The body is an asset for us in every way. It is who we are.

free

'COS I'M FREE

Consider, if you will, the zoo. The zoo of today has changed radically from the zoo of my childhood. Taronga Zoo in Sydney used to be a landscape of pits and cages—a territory of walls and iron bars. The animals paced up and down, going mad with boredom.

I vividly remember visiting the female elephant. She kept swaying back and forth like a giant pendulum—back and forth, back and forth—as though she had some sort of behavioural tic. Something about being in the zoo had destroyed her soul. Today, at huge cost, the zoo has 'enclosures' and 'displays', not cages and pits. The enclosures and displays are an attempt to give the impression of nature and freedom. Why? Because visitors to zoos couldn't stomach what a previous generation could. We find zoos with animals in cages nauseating because we can't imagine anything worse than living in a cage ourselves. After all, how do we punish criminals? By removing the most precious thing they have: their liberty.

There's nothing we want more than our freedom. At least, it's hard to think what we could want more than that. Many thinkers have suggested that freedom is what makes us truly human. Freedom is something we have naturally, like feet and bellybutton fluff.

According to the 'Declaration of the Rights of Man and of the Citizen' which was drawn up and approved at the dawn of the French Revolution, "Men are born and remain free".[20] Or, if you like your philosophy a little less highbrow, Mel Gibson (playing the Scottish hero William Wallace in *Braveheart*) gargled to his soldiers, "They may take our lives, but they may never take our freedom!"—and was promptly cut down by the English.

Freedom is a powerful idea—an idea of such power, it makes us think of glorious stories about the overthrowing of tyrants and empires, the fight against slavery, and the pursuit of women's and workers' rights. Freedom is a cause worth fighting for.

INDIVIDUALIZED

Whatever the glories of freedom's past causes, individual freedom has become a shadow of its former self. Freedom used to mean something noble—the freedom to live without the government watching you all the time, the freedom to speak, the freedom to believe. But now freedom mostly means the freedom to buy.

Our prophets of freedom are not great heroes like Martin Luther King Jr and Gandhi; they are the entertainment industry and the engines of global commerce. Individual freedom has now been reduced to sex and shopping—the unbridled consumption of people and things—the quest for the perfect orgasm and the best pair of shoes. Now, as more than one sociologist has pointed out, we are what we consume: I shop, therefore I am.

UNDERPANTS ON THE OUTSIDE

There is another aspect of freedom that usually lies hidden: too often, our freedom comes at the expense of the freedom of others. In other words, securing our personal liberties has pretty much meant making others into slaves. The project of freedom has a definite dark side.

This has happened in two ways. Firstly, the First World has historically grown fat on the increased impoverishment of the Third World. The Nike swoosh logo means self-expression, exhilarating athleticism and success to us, but for many years, it has meant virtual slavery to the children who have made your running shoes for a pittance. Secondly, our endless summer of consumption cannot possibly be sustained by the finite resources of the earth without some consequences. And we are only now beginning to discover how serious the climatic consequences might be.

We can see that holding to unqualified freedom as the thing we most desire is deeply troublesome because of the results it produces. But there's an even deeper problem: to insist that a person is only truly free when every aspect of his/her life is a matter of choice between available alternatives is really to understand freedom as a rejection of finiteness. Choice is what makes us believe we are gods. 'A man's got to know his limitations', and modern men and women don't know theirs. Ultimate freedom (or so we dream) is the path to immortality. What a rude surprise to find the rug pulled out from under our feet! We think we can fly if we just wear our underpants on the outside, and yet the ground is rushing up fast to meet us.

THE TASKS OF FREEDOM

Freedom, as we first received it, wasn't a moral thing. The first people were given freedom for a purpose—for a job: to bring the creation to its potential. It was a gift from their maker to use and enjoy.

We see this in Genesis 2 when God brings the animals to Adam "to see what he would call them" (v. 19). Naming something is a remarkable privilege: it means being allowed the responsibility of seeing into the essence of things and giving them a label. Whatever Adam called the animal, that was its name. God did not decide the names beforehand and then play a game of Twenty Questions with the man.

Adam and Eve were also freed for the task of tilling and keeping the ground—of so ordering the garden that it flourished and produced a crop. They were to exercise their freedom not in domination, but in tender dominion—realizing the potential latent in the good but not yet perfected world in which they had been placed.

They were also free to enjoy all the rich goodness of the creation. They were free to eat of any tree in the garden in any order, or not at all. They could pig out on apples but stay away from avocadoes—if that was their choice. They could also abstain from pears but gorge themselves on figs—if that was their choice.

They were also freed for each other. No longer lonely, they were open in their nakedness to relish the unity of their flesh, and to share the task of filling the creation with people. Human freedom has always been social.

But their freedom was always limited. They were limited, of course, by their physiology: they were like the animals, made from the dust of the ground, and they could only be in one place at a time. Unlike the one who made them, they could only create out of the materials he had given them. But knowing their limitations was their freedom.

Their liberty was also limited in another important way: they were not free to eat of the tree of the knowledge of good and evil. God warned them as much as commanded them: "You may surely eat of every tree of the garden, but of the tree of the knowledge of good and evil you shall not eat, for in the day that you eat of it you shall surely die" (Gen 2:16-17).

DECLARATION OF INDEPENDENCE

The decision of Adam and Eve to eat this fruit was not a march for freedom but a choice for chains. With their fall came new limits on human freedom. The creation was shot through with decay. The earth no longer yields so readily to our touch. Our relationships are riddled with shame and the abusive domination of males over females.

The ultimate boundary on human freedom—the final crushing blow to our egotism—is death. Despite our fantasies, we cannot break free of the gravity—the *grave*-ity—of death. We may go "gentle into that good night" or even "rage against the dying of the light",[21] but our destiny remains unchanged. Death is the termination of all decisions. Despite all your rage, you are still "just a rat in a cage" (to quote the Smashing Pumpkins).[22]

And we are not free to change. We have lost the capacity to realize the potential within ourselves for doing what we were made to do. We are bound to the flesh, sold as slaves to sin, not even able to do the good we want to do (Rom 5-7). No amount of self-help can help. It is no use following rules as a strategy for freedom; the laws in the Bible were like the arrows on a convict's uniform pointing to our lack of freedom rather than giving us directions for escape.

THE FREE MAN

We are born free, but everywhere we are in chains. It is like we can see the summer holidays ahead of us, but every day is a boring old day in November.

But Jesus was free. He was free to be the man he was created to be. Somehow he was not a prisoner to his habits and vices, desires and appetites.

How did he use this freedom? By voluntarily submitting to the restrictions and indignities of human flesh—living in a family, making use of the tongue and lips he now possessed to learn human language, putting up with the need to sleep and eat, resigning himself to being a creature flowing with hormones and blood, facing the possibility of death. As a man, he exercised the freedom of a true human being—authority without domination, care without exploitation—and offered his own body for the sake of others. In his absolute liberty, he didn't seek stardom or pursue fame and fortune. Instead, in humility, he went to the cross to bear the shame of all and to give his life freely as a ransom for many—not demanding the servitude of others, but instead embracing slavery *for* others.

LIVING IN FREEDOM

True freedom, then, comes from faith. Faith releases us from the bleak destiny of sin and death into new life as the children of God. Paul explains that belonging to Christ is not slavery to law or to religious observance, but freedom to love: "For freedom Christ has set us free", he says in Galatians 5:1. In other words, we have been freed for the purpose of embracing the freedom we were made for as God's creatures—the freedom we lost through sin. Now we have been set free from sin, condemnation and death by Christ. The people of God are not a community framed by dos and don'ts; they are a community moulded by freedom.

However, like many prisoners, we grow to love our cages. It was hard for the early Christians to accept that they had been released; it was easier to imagine staying put within the safety of the law—much like the long-term inmate who, after being discharged, commits a crime so that he can return to prison where there are things like regular meals. The life of freedom is far more scary. You need to use your imaginative powers to love rather than follow a set of rules. Circumcision would be easier.

And so Paul writes in Galatians 5:13:

> For you were called to freedom, brothers. Only do not use your freedom as an opportunity for the flesh, but through love serve one another.

The Greek word 'serve' contains the idea of slavery—that is, through love, *become slaves to one another*. At the core of the Christian life is a freedom that is—surprisingly—exercised in costly service to others. As Martin Luther put it, "A Christian man is the most free lord of all, and subject to none; a Christian man is the most dutiful servant of all, and subject to every one."[23] To become a Christian, then, is to become a slave. That's a strange thing to say, isn't it!

---

5 COMMENTS

Bec   But as long as we are under the rule of some authority, are we ever really free? And if there is no authority, wouldn't there be anarchy? Anarchy isn't really a state of freedom. So is there such a thing as freedom?

Michael	Well, that's an interesting question. One of the problems is we see authority and freedom as opposites when, in fact, authority is needed for freedom to flourish. Can you play tennis without a net?
Byron	I think it's called squash.
Justin	▶ *"We are what we consume".* Yes. But don't you perceive a backlash against this—even in completely secular circles? Aren't many people tired of this kind of 'freedom'—even if they do not know how to get out of it?
Mike	Nice insight here about where our freedom march attempts to go (i.e. to immortality). Notice how our society allows us to remove our own freedom willingly. So I can mess up my life any way I want by making choices that limit my freedom. But as soon as someone else encroaches on my freedom, lo and behold, it's the end of freedom as we know it.

stuff

YOU AND YOUR STUFF

I got up one morning to write, and sat down facing the Three Sisters, that famous rock formation in the Blue Mountains near Sydney. The feeling you get when you look down that ancient valley is quite spooky. The thrusting fingers of sheer rock poke defiantly at the sky. They seem oblivious of the weather, and the shifts in animal and plant life around them.

But the truth is, of course, that the Three Sisters are nothing more than huge sandcastles. They are falling down—eroding away little by little, blowing away in the wind. Even though they have the appearance of agelessness and permanence, they are temporary.

This illustrates something quite well: the world of stuff—though good and beautiful, solid and graspable—won't last forever. God rules and is sovereign over stuff. He controls stuff: he gives it and he takes it away; he makes it and he destroys it; he arranges it and he scatters it.

It can be frustrating to try to love God. "He is so—well—invisible", as someone said in my Bible Study group once. How hard is it to love an invisible being?

On the other hand, the world of things seems so much more real—concrete—solid—tangible. The world we can sense seems so much more *alive*. At least I can have certainty that my car, my iPod and my overseas holiday exist. As physical creatures, we yearn for connection with the physical world. The non-physical seems second-order.

TO HAVE AND TO HOLD

It seems sensible to us wealthy westerners to have faith in the stuff we can grasp, rather than in the idea of God. Believing in God causes crazy behaviour—like blowing up people who are just trying to enjoy their piece of the sensual world. The having of possessions gives us power and status and authority; it makes us a higher order of beings on this planet.

In our culture, the idea of property and the idea of possessions is sacred. The stuff that is mine is spiritually bonded to me: it has existence and meaning because of me (its owner) because I designate it to be so. My stuff is an extension of my self. We are gods of our stuff. To steal my stuff is to violate me. Can you imagine what it's like to lose everything you have? I know someone for whom this occurred: it all went because of a bushfire in 1994. I also heard about a guy in the UK who was moving house. He packed everything he owned (and I mean everything) into a truck and drove it up to Manchester. He parked it outside a pub while he went to have a beer over lunch, and then afterwards came back to find that—you guessed it—the truck had gone. It had been stolen. We shouldn't take this devastating loss of stuff lightly.

What possession would it most break your heart to lose? Your iPod? Your car? Your wedding ring? When we moved from Australia to the UK, we got rid of heaps of our stuff. Lots of it we put on the pavement outside our inner city house, and people just stopped, picked it up and took it away: old computers, wardrobes, knick-knacks, children ... (no, just kidding!). It's amazing what people will take. At first it was a wrench, but then it felt strangely liberating to be free of so much stuff.

For its part, the Bible offers a radical challenge to our love of and attachment to stuff, without saying that stuff itself is bad. The Bible's got two angles on stuff: firstly, stuff is temporary, whereas God is eternal; and secondly, God is the giver of stuff.

MY PRECIOUS ...

The illusion of permanence in stuff is powerful, but stuff is just rearranged dust. The world of the material is a shifting kaleidoscope of molecules and atoms. The writer of the book of Ecclesiastes (who tells us he is a man of impressive wealth) has plenty to say about this:

> There is a grievous evil that I have seen under the sun: riches were kept by their owner to his hurt, and those riches were lost in a bad venture. And he is father of a son, but he has nothing in his hand. As he came from his mother's womb he shall go again, naked as he came, and shall take nothing for his toil that he may carry away in his hand. This also is a grievous evil: just as he came, so shall he go, and what gain is there to him who toils for the wind? (Eccl 5:13-16)

Our attachment to stuff is only temporary. Our lives result in a zero sum gain. We come nude, we leave nude (but usually with more wrinkles). Our hearts are attracted by stuff but stuff frustrates us. We grasp at it with slippery fingers, partly because we are stuff too.

There is also a pretty strong challenge to the allure of wealth in the Psalms:

> Be not afraid when a man becomes rich,
>   when the glory of his house increases.
> For when he dies he will carry nothing away;
>   his glory will not go down after him.
> For though, while he lives, he counts himself blessed
>   —and though you get praise when you do well for
>   yourself—
> his soul will go to the generation of his fathers,
>   who will never again see light.
> Man in his pomp yet without understanding is like the
>   beasts that perish. (Ps 49:16-20)

Our own impermanence makes our link to stuff meaningless and foolish. You have heard it said that "The one who dies with the most toys wins"; I say to you that "The one who dies with the most stuff still dies". Ultimately, an encounter with God is the destination of every traveller, and we need to travel light.

Jesus in his Sermon on the Mount challenges us even further:

> "Do not lay up for yourselves treasures on earth, where moth and rust destroy and where thieves break in and steal, but lay up for yourselves treasures in heaven, where neither moth nor rust destroys and where thieves do not break in and steal. For where your treasure is, there your heart will be also." (Matt 6:19-21)

We are like Gollum sometimes. Remember that hideous creature from *The Lord of the Rings*? He hid away with his ring, holding it close to his heart and calling it his "precious". But ultimately the ring ruled him—corrupted him—made him a monster—and the loss of it totally destroyed him.

Are you like Gollum? Are you possessed by your possessions? What is your "precious"? Where, then, is your heart?

NAKED I CAME ...

Stuff is temporary (whereas God is eternal), but God is the giver of stuff. Why? Because as the creator of all things, he ultimately owns all stuff. It comes from him. He rules it. We are only leaseholders or trustees.

God being the giver of stuff means that stuff is good, by the way. Genesis 1 records God's verdict on creation—that it was "good", "good", "good", "good", "good" and "very good". Paul writes "For everything created by God is good, and nothing is to be rejected if it is received with thanksgiving, for it is made holy by the word of God and prayer" (1 Tim 4:4-5). So stuff isn't bad. But it ain't God, either. Only God is God.

So if we have stuff, it is on loan. The Israelites were told to remember this when they went in and took possession of the land of Israel—that the stuff they would be enjoying was not something they had earned themselves but it had been given to them as a gift from God (Deut 6:10-15). We convince ourselves that we earn the rights to stuff, but we don't remember that the ability and circumstances that lead to our ownership of stuff have been given to us. All that we have is gifted. What would it look like in your life if you treated everything you own as a gift, not as yours by right?

We should also remember that God's rule over stuff means that he may choose to remove our stuff. You might remember Job, a wealthy man who enjoyed prosperity. God chose to remove all his wealth, burning up his property, his livestock and his possessions. What was Job's response?

"Naked I came from my mother's womb, and naked shall I return. The LORD gave, and the LORD has taken away; blessed be the name of the LORD." (Job 1:21)

God rules stuff. He can give it, and he can take it away. If you have stuff, be thankful. But don't presume that it's your right. Receive stuff with thankfulness. What would it look like in practical terms if we lived as if all our stuff was a gift?

7 COMMENTS

Drew | It's never just stuff, is it? So much of what matters to us—particularly when life is hard—is not stuff you can put your finger or your foot on: love, friendship, fun, feelings, dreams, memories, regrets.

Michael | Or, to put it the other way round, somehow we human beings can't help but attach these meanings to our stuff. So we value things because they represent the more valuable things we can't hold onto—for example, family photos, or the souvenir from a holiday. These are the things we would choose to rescue if our houses burnt down.

Byron | Some of my stuff may be part of a relationship with another: it either facilitates my relationship with another person and makes it happen (for example, my computer helps me to connect with others through email, instant messager), or it symbolizes it (for example, my wedding ring symbolizes the promises I made to my wife on our wedding day). I suspect you would say similar things in this case (e.g. avoid idolatry through being grateful). Still, it's interesting that 'stuff' isn't just about me and God; it *can* be (and, in fact, it often is) about me, you and God.

Michael | Yes, there's owning and there's giving, but there's also sharing, which is a different kind of relationship to stuff. It's a tie to a thing that depends on us trusting each other to work.

Bec

> *"What would it look like in your life if you treated everything you own as a gift, not as yours by right?"*

Maybe I wouldn't be so precious about it!

Mim

In practical terms, if I lived as if all my stuff was a gift from God, I would be in awe of my stuff, and would tell everyone about my stuff and about the one who gave it to me. I would share and lend my stuff and give my stuff away. I would respect my stuff and really be grateful for it.

Michael

Thankfulness seems to me to be a way in which a whole life can be lived. It could be a theme—a motto—an 'attitude of gratitude', perhaps.

Thankfulness is a way to receive gifts. It is a happy receiving of them, but it also involves the use of these gifts precisely as gifts. It's a different way of possessing things.

speech, speech!

It took a team of philologists, aided by a bizarre crew of amateur crackpots, 68 years (from 1860 to 1928) to compile the *Oxford English Dictionary* in a house not far from where I am sitting now. It has over half a million entries, and needs the best part of a standard-sized bookcase to contain its 22 or so volumes. The word 'set' alone takes 37 pages to explain. And, of course, it needs revising every generation or so as new words, and new meanings for old words, spring up out of everywhere: 'smog', 'text message', 'wicked', 'Mcjob', 'bootylicious' and so on.

An extraordinary amount of effort has gone into attempting to classify and control human language because, while language is one of the most glorious gifts of humanity, it is also tricky, inexact and potentially dangerous. Words have more power than bombs. The old playground adage "Sticks and stones may break my bones, but names will never hurt me" is patently false: labels can wound deeply and cause festering sores that never heal. With words, you can shape the way whole peoples think about the world or about other people. With words, tanks, planes and guns are commanded. With words, contracts and treaties are drawn up and ratified. Words like 'collateral' and 'damage', once put together, are designed to minimize the negative impact of civilian casualties in war. Words are essential to our capacity to relate to one another, nation to nation, individual to individual. By speaking to one another, we are capable of a profound intimacy with one another that even the dolphins never know.

For its part, the Bible claims that because we are built for relationship with God our maker, we speak. We of all the creatures are most like him. He creates specifically by talking the universe into being: he says, and it is so. He allows Adam to name the animals. Perhaps, then, there is nothing more basically human than the act—and the art—of communicating through words.

THE BROKEN SIGN

But the corruption of the world began with words—words that were false. And so, along with everything else, language became corrupted. Words became the bearers of destruction, as well as of creation—weapons of war, as well as instruments of healing. We now have lies, broken promises, half-truths, pieces of gossip, whinges, boasts, taunts, curses, nagging, libel, slander, flattery, demeaning and debased talk, bullying and cynical criticism.

We have also lost control of our words. With speech, humanity is a bit like a gorilla with a loaded pistol: an explosive weapon lies in the hands of someone who has an uncertain control over it. While, on the one hand, we know that our words have immense power to do harm or to do good, on the other hand, we are not always masters of what we say: the words just slip out ...

WISE WORDS

On the other hand, God is a talking God—a God who uses words to create, to promise, to love and to communicate. He describes the world as it really is, without lies or tricks. He calls on us to turn to him, and then sends his Son—the one they call the word of God—in the flesh to walk among us, full of grace and truth (John 1:1, 14).

In his death, Jesus announced that mercy is available to all who believe in the promises of God. He brings us together into a new group of people who now face a new task. Instead of using words to tear each other down or serve personal ambition, we are to speak *God's* words—both to the world and to each other—out of reverent fear of him. Being the God who is love and the God who is true, God is honoured by words that are loving and true.

Since using words and talking are such basic activities for human beings, it is not surprising that the Bible has much to say on the subject—particularly in the book of Proverbs. Proverbs is a book on wise living, and its advice to us is "If you really want to honour the Lord, watch your words carefully".

For example, take Proverbs 18:21: "Death and life are in the power of the tongue, and those who love it will eat its fruits". This verse is saying that words have immense destructive power. It is amazing how easily you can shatter a person's self-confidence with a put-down. The damaging words of a tired and irritated parent may be remembered by their child forever. However, the tongue can also deliver words that cause people to flourish. What does the second part of the proverb mean? The word 'fruits' refers to what comes about from what is said. In Proverbs, 'fruit' is usually a positive association. So I think it's highlighting that if you regard the tongue well and speak wisely, you will reap the rewards.

Or take Proverbs 12:18: "There is one whose rash words are like sword thrusts, but the tongue of the wise brings healing". Unthinking words can cause deep wounds, piercing like a sword. But you know when a wise person speaks because of the healing effects their words bring: relationships flourish, people blossom through encouragement and comfort, and peace reigns.

LIES, LIES, LIES

In our time, people are pessimistic about the value of words. Words have been corrupted by the lies of politicians, journalists and scientists—by the betrayals of lovers and the falsity of parents—and, most of all, by the incessant braying of advertising. People think that if there is no God to answer to, you can lie with impunity. No-one underwrites words; you can't bank on them to mean what they appear to mean. Not so long ago, a former US President famously said, "I did not have sex with that woman"—by which he pretty much meant, "I did have sex with that woman".

We do not trust words because we do not trust the people who use them. Everything is spin. No promise is credible. This is partly why people have lost faith in marriage as an ideal: my 'yes' can mean 'maybe', and my 'until death do us part' can mean 'until I've had enough'. But too many promises have been broken ...

BRAGGING, FLATTERY, GOSSIP

There are other vices of speech, too—for example, bragging: "Let another praise you, and not your own mouth; a stranger, and not your own lips" (Prov 27:2). Australian culture has always had a kind of anti-bragging thing going. However, as we become more success-oriented, and as we continue to place the famous and the high-achieving on higher and higher pedestals, we develop more of an acceptance of self-promotion and arrogance. If I don't sell myself, who will?

Flattery is another bad habit of the tongue: "A lying tongue hates its victims, and a flattering mouth works ruin" (Prov 26:28). Flattery, you see, is a form of deceit: the flatterer lays on the compliments in order to achieve his own purposes. Flatter the boss and you will get a promotion. Flatter that girl and she will find you attractive. That's the difference between genuine encouragement (which serves another) and flattery (which serves the self): flattery is manipulative.

And then there is gossip. We all love to do it. But Proverbs 11:13 says, "A gossip betrays a confidence, but a trustworthy man keeps a secret" (NIV). This verse is almost a dictionary definition—a statement of a fact. It shows how much more appealing it is to be friends with the trustworthy person instead of with the gossip. Gossiping is extremely difficult to control because it is recreational. Yet the key word in this proverb is the word 'betrays': gossip is so awful because it is poisonous to loving relationships.

IN PRAISE OF PRAISE

As we have seen, in the wrong mouths, words can wreak devastation. But the remarkable thing is that God chooses to use human words in his salvation plan for the world. God gives us words about himself so that we can know him. He gives us words about him so that we might, in turn, use our words to praise him. He enables people to talk about him with their limited human words—and do more than just talk about him. God uses human words to bring about his mighty purposes—to advance the redemption of the world and even to give life to the dead!

The power of words proves to be very positive. We have words that help us to adopt God's perspective and not remain hemmed in by our immediate circumstances. Words are good at transcending time and space: they help us remember and look forward–to "seek the things that are above" (Col 3:1). Words can make us see with our mind's eye, hear with our mind's ears and even smell with our mind's noses. Words are not merely conveyances for concepts (though they do that job too). The Bible itself is our model, illustrating just how rich language describing the things of God ought to be and has to be.

So the purpose for which our tongues were made is praising our creator and saying the things he wants said.

11 COMMENTS

Byron	Is it more human to speak or to listen? Perhaps the latter if we are the recipients of God's words before we become imitators of him in speech (Gen 1:26: "Let us make man in our image").
Michael	Yes. Two ears, one mouth, as they say. 'Respond' is a good word to use here. That's what we do: we respond. Responding can mean hearing and talking ...
Byron	*"The words just slip out ..."* Unfortunately, not all slips of the tongue are accidental. Often the most hurtful things are the lies made in cold blood, the insult crafted with both eyes open, the blasphemy uttered with a heart of stone ...
Michael	Indeed. I guess one of the weird things about being able to talk is how almost everyone has said things they didn't want to say at some point: "Me and my big mouth ..."

Simon   I reckon the power of God's words is definitely seen in creation. However, to see the power of words, we only need look in Genesis 3 and the effect that Satan's words had on Eve. Eve chose to react to those words and, in doing so, sinned against God.

Words have power to affect other people's thinking. They have the power to lead people to act rightly, but also to act sinfully. God's loving, forgiving words are words to cherish and model our life on—especially in our relationships with the ones we love!

Often we need to remember that what we say matters—sometimes because we're not used to being listened to. The power of words is found in someone listening.

Jeltzz   For all the lies, people have not abandoned words. Words are still the currency of communicative life. They are the bread and water we cannot escape. The reaction to lies is more 'spin', but spin is nothing new; we have always constructed our reality with language. We present truth with nuance, and we use shading to reveal some things while surreptitiously casting others into darkness.

The basis of all lies is truth. Deception is parasitic by nature. We function with an assumption of honesty, even when we apply deep scepticism to our acts of listening.

Michael   Yes, lies wouldn't be successful if we didn't believe them—if we weren't trusting by nature. We can't live without trust, so we will even believe a lie if it helps us get along.

Lynne   And even when we're sceptical, no communication is possible unless there's an underlying assumption that most of it is true. It's almost like (and not being a philosopher here, I'm probably using the wrong terms) there's an unspoken social contract there: we expect communication to reflect some level of reality, and untruth is a violation of that expectation. (Of course, in a cynical society, the 'contract' has broken down in certain areas—for example, tax returns, political statements. But in our everyday relationships, most of us, I hope, still have higher expectations.)

Joanna   There's just something rotten about the way our society is structured, with the volume of gossip you know indicating your 'coolness' and importance to the 'inner circle' of whatever your circle is. The problem is, this causes anyone who wants to feel important (and therefore loved) to gossip. Now, hands up all the people who don't want to feel important!

Sarah   Regardless of whether it's our mouths or ears that offend, gossip foams out of some ignoble spot down deep that quietly sighs when it's someone else getting bullied or trashed. We euphemistically call it 'chit chat' and 'girl talk' and 'fellowship', and say things like, "Let's all bow our heads and pray for Mary who's having a really hard time of it because blah, blah, blah ..." Even when gossip doesn't particularly offend, it's a bit like a dirty emission that degrades the environment. At worst, it's a cowardly attack against the defenseless and a cunning way to ensure that someone other than me is on the outside wanting in.

Honoria   I've been searching for a good definition of gossip. Labelling something as 'gossip' is a subjective business. I quite like my pastor's wife's definition: giving information for your own sake, (sometimes) at the expense of the subject of the gossip. Here, the motivation is self-aggrandizement—self-promotion—making yourself look good. Gossip is more than a matter of truthfulness, scope, volume, privacy, helpfulness, malice or appropriateness (although exercising wisdom in speech means considering these elements). But the words we speak need to be congruent with Christian service—that is, grounded in loving other person-centredness.

child

MOTHER'S DAY

How do you celebrate Mother's Day? It may be a day of joy for your family; it may be a day of grief. But even if you never become a parent yourself, you will always have a reason to celebrate Mother's Day. It's more universal than Christmas. You never stop being a child of your parents. After life, being a child is one of the things all human beings share, biologically and sociologically. (Usually the contributors of our genetic material are also the ones who bring us up, but this is not always the case—for example, in blended families, or in families that have adopted children.) As the Bible puts it, filling the earth (i.e. with children) was one of the tasks given to the original couple (Gen 1:28). We've done this pretty well (although Antarctica has proven to be a tough one ...).

It is not surprising, then, that the Ten Commandments that God gave to Moses in the Old Testament mentions parents and how they are to be treated, and that this passage is directed to people of any age. The fifth commandment is this: "Honor your father and your mother, that your days may be long in the land that the LORD your God is giving you" (Exod 20:12; cf. Deut 5:16). But what does it mean?

Often we view parental influence as a gravity we have to struggle against with all our might to escape. Certainly Eminem thought so. Here's part of his 'apology' to his mother, 'Cleanin' Out My Closet':

> Now I would never diss my own mama just to get recognition
> Take a second to listen for who you think this record is dissing
> But put yourself in my position, just try to envision
> Witnessing your mama popping prescription pills in the
>   kitchen ...

> But how dare you try to take what you didn't help me to get
> You selfish ****, I hope you **** burn in hell for this ****!
> Remember when Ronnie died and you said you wished it was
>   me?
> Well guess what, I am dead, dead to you as can be ...

> I'm sorry, mama
> I never meant to hurt you
> I never meant to make you cry
> But tonight, I'm cleaning out my closet ...[24]

Neither of Eminem's parents was ideal. He 'cleans out his closet' by listing his grievances against his mother and his disappearing dad. At the end of this tirade, he curses his mother and severs the relationship completely: "I am dead, dead to you as can be". And who can blame him? His anger is real and it sounds justified.

HONOUR

What about honour? How do you honour your parents? In the Bible's terms, honouring them means giving them the respect and dignity they are due, and listening to their wisdom and teaching.

After all, dispensing wisdom and teaching is part of a parent's role. They don't just supply sperm and ova; they act as givers of life and wisdom. Parents are to instruct their children in how to live well—by word and by example. So in the book of Proverbs we are encouraged to "Listen to your father who gave you life, and do not despise your mother when she is old" (Prov 23:22). We are also warned that:

> The eye that mocks a father
>   and scorns to obey a mother
> will be picked out by the ravens of the valley
>   and eaten by the vultures. (Prov 30:17)

Okay, already! I think we get the point: ignoring the wisdom of your parents leads to ruin.

Don't think about this like it's karma—that is, if you bag your parents, it will return to you by some mystical energy. It is just an observation—a truth about the way things are. Honouring your parents is a wise strategy.

Parents have been given a spiritual mission from God to teach and nurture their young. God has put them in a position of authority over their children and bestowed on them the responsibility to care for and grow their offspring.

Parental authority comes from the fact that parents are God's representatives to their children. In their parenting of us, they mimic God himself. This is the centre of the biblical idea of parenthood: God alone is properly, truly and primarily parent/ Father. No human parents really create their child or control his or her destiny; all they do is have sex! God is the true giver of life; parents are merely the guardians he appoints of that life. And because this reflects God's own parenthood of us, human parenthood ought to be celebrated and honoured. God is the true teacher—the true wisdom—the ultimate life guide. Human parents follow after him. They are to imitate God. In addition, just as parents are to imitate God in their parenting, children are called to honour God by honouring their parents.

PLEASE DON'T MENTION THE OUTSIDE WORLD

'Parents', I reckon, can include your biological mother and father but also anybody involved in the whole bringing of You up. Teachers, for example, act legally *in loco parentis*—that is, 'in the place of parents'. As they perform this task, I reckon they deserve a piece of the honour. This may be true of other mentors in our lives—'uncles' and 'aunties', grandparents, youth leaders, sports coaches, and so on.

Of course, what this honour means in concrete terms will differ with the age of the child. For a small child, honouring his or her parents is mainly about being obedient and cooperative. From 12 to 18, it gets a little more complicated as we get caught between striving for independence and clinging to the dependence of living under the roof of our parents. For the young man or young woman, bringing honour to your parents may not mean allowing them absolute control; it may mean negotiating with them in a mature and sensible fashion about things like a curfew and when you can use the car. Even when you are no longer a child, it will mean being a credit to them in who you are in your character as a human being—having a reputation that honours them.

The obligation we have to honour our parents never ceases. Much as we don't like to admit it, our parents remain our parents even when we become adults or parents ourselves. An elderly person with attentive and loving children and grandchildren is blessed indeed. The old folks' home on *The Simpsons* shows the opposite: at Thanksgiving, the manager reads out a few lame faxes from families who "wished they could be here today". Yeah, right! No wonder the sign on the door says "Thank you for not discussing the outside world". When we are adults, just because our parents are old doesn't mean we can't honour them, even though the relationship has changed.

WOMAN, BEHOLD, YOUR SON!

Bearing in mind that parents were given their authority from God in the first place, of course it is ultimately God we must obey, not parents (though hopefully these will coincide as the purpose of parenthood is to point us to God's rule over us anyway). This is a radical idea because it means it is possible for there to be times when honouring your parents looks like something they don't immediately recognize. The son of a thief honours his father by ignoring his father's urgings to steal. The daughter of a drunkard honours her mother by not sharing her drinking binges.

Obviously, there will always be parents who are weak, foolish, self-seeking, tyrannical, abusive, neglectful and corrupt. Human parents, even though they have been given authority from God, are just human—like their children. They are not morally or physically superior.

So how do I honour my parents who are just human like me? Well, firstly, we need to recognize they're only human. Some of the greatest evils of the human race have been committed by parents towards their children. I once read a book by psychiatrist M Scott Peck which talked about an 11-year-old boy whose parents gave him the gun his elder brother had shot himself earlier with as a Christmas present.[25] That kind of evil leaves you speechless.

In fact, one mistake you might make is viewing your human parents as being perfect, not recognizing their sins and limitations. I have seen adult children who are far too dependent on their parents for material things and opinions. It is almost dishonouring to the parents that their children haven't been able to grow free of parental influence.

Honouring your parents is not a contradiction of God's command. This means that you can honour your parents even when they fail you. And if human parents fail, the Fatherhood of God becomes all the more significant to us because he is the perfect and true parent of us all. Think of the father in the story of the lost son (or prodigal son) in Luke's Gospel: he was waiting with open arms and tear-stained face for the return of his wayward boy (Luke 15:11-31).

And if we need a model of how to be a child, we need look no further than Jesus who honoured his human parents even though he was far greater than them, and who always obeyed the will of his heavenly Father even in great trial and agony— to the point of separation.

When Jesus was 12, he caused his human parents great concern. While they were starting their journey home, he was debating in the temple with the rather gobsmacked religious teachers, displaying his prodigious powers of understanding the Scriptures (Luke 2:41-50). I imagine that Mary and Joseph were none too pleased to discover his absence. It took them three days to find him, and when they did, his mother chided him: "Son, why have you treated us so? Behold, your father and I have been searching for you in great distress" (Luke 2:48). Our sympathy as human beings is with them, isn't it? Of course they were worried! (Although, to search Jerusalem—which wasn't, at the time, a huge metropolis by any means—without looking in the most significant public building, the one that dominated the city, is kind of odd, in my opinion.)

But Jesus answered them by saying, "Why were you looking for me? Did you not know that I must be in my Father's house?" (Luke 2:49). He sounded a little cheeky, perhaps, but Jesus knew that his first allegiance as a child belonged to his heavenly Father, not his earthly parents. Anyway, Luke goes on to record that Jesus was obedient—"submissive" (Luke 2:51)—to his parents after that. Bizarre isn't it? How strange that the mighty Son of God humbled himself and became obedient even to fallible human parents like Mary and Joseph!

Then, as Jesus hung dying on the cross, one of things he remembered to do was to take care of his mum. John tells us that Jesus, upon seeing Mary standing there alongside one of his disciples, said to her, "Woman, behold, your son!", and to the disciple, "Behold, your mother!" From then on, she became part of that man's household (John 19:26-27).

SOME LAST WORDS

It wasn't long ago that two friends of mine, Tim and Carli, each lost a father to cancer within a week of each other. I went to two funerals in three days. Both Tim and Carli were given a chance to say a few words about their dads.

At the time, Tim had been a Christian for only a few months. He spoke with humour, love and respect about his dad, not neglecting his faults, but honouring him and thanking God for his life. In front of his non-Christian family, he spoke of his own faith, and of his hope that his dad had given his life to Jesus in his last hours.

Carli also spoke eloquently and affectionately about her dad.

She remembered her struggles with him as well as the happier times. She spoke with confidence about how, in his last months, her dad had come to know Jesus Christ.

I was blown away by how these people honoured their fathers and so gave the glory to God the Father.

8 COMMENTS

Anonymous
You can hate stuff about your parents, and acknowledge that, and still love them. It's healthy, in fact. If a parent has died, it can be hard to reconcile bad memories of them or things you did not like about them with the feeling you are disrespecting them by having these feelings. But, like any relationship, you can have both: things you can't stand and an overwhelming sense of love.

I agree that a public 'dissing' of the parentals Eminem-style is not honouring them. But private acknowledgement can be good.

Bjem
A recent report here in the USA claimed the most common thing American fathers say to their children is "Be quiet!" Without trying to sound too 'Cat's in the Cradle'-ish, it's interesting to think about kids growing up to be just like their parents. Is this where "it may go well for [us]" (Deut 5:16) when we establish habits of honouring others?

Can someone define biblical honouring? Wiktionary says: "to honour: 1. to think of highly, to respect highly; 2. to confer honour upon (someone)".[26] Michael, are you using it in this way?

Michael
Yes, honouring is an act of communication. It carries a message. It can be something you say or something you do, but it has a particular meaning—in this case, that the person is given worth or glory or praise in some way.

Actually, praise isn't quite right; it is more like they are given the dignity that is their due.

Anonymous This is kind of a tangent, but it was a light bulb for me the other day. I was talking to someone about earthly parents and having God as a Father. This person had a parent with a mental illness and, as a result, he was left to his own devices and was never disciplined. We read in Hebrews 12 that if you are God's child, he disciplines you; it is a mark of being his child—loved by God, not hated!

Furthermore, he disciplines us for our good. This is so different to a lot of kids' experience of 'discipline' (especially in abusive situations), where discipline is a result of a parent's anger or sin, rather than the good of the child being the primary motivator. (Of course, this is not really discipline at all.) I am a parent, and I am going to try and remember to discipline for my child's good, not out of my anger or frustration. God is good!

Byron Part of what it means to honour our parents is for us to be for our children what our parents were for us. Not that we are to repeat their mistakes (though it can be difficult to avoid that!), but that we become the bearers of tradition, passing on their wisdom and the idea of what it means to be human—to be You.

This doesn't exclude single people. They might not have the opportunity to pass on tradition by being a parent, but that doesn't rule them out of shaping the next generation in other contexts (e.g. Sunday school, mentoring).

I find this idea fascinating, though it certainly doesn't exhaust the scope of what 'honour' means.

Rachel I love the old concept of 'it takes a village to raise a child'. I read somewhere that part of the reason parent/child relationships are often stuffed in modern-day western society is due to the individualization of society and the notion that those who raise/know/understand you the best should be your biological parents.

Rhea

> *"Just as parents are to imitate God in their parenting, children are called to honour God by honouring their parents."*

I like this. I wouldn't want to go beyond this—particularly with abusive parents. Any discussion about this topic needs to be qualified by the standard of behaviour that God expects of parents so that those of us who have it tough aren't under even more guilt. If my parents are abusive, how can I honour them? How should I act towards them?

Michael

Well, there are parallels with living with a tyrannical and corrupt ruler. Honouring parents can take many forms depending on who your parents are. How one's parents might be honoured needs to be worked out in each situation. It may well be honouring to a parent to take them to the police, for instance.

boy/girl

THE GREAT DISINTEGRATION

> And the man and his wife were both naked and were not
> ashamed. (Gen 2:25)

Today everything is all about sex. Oh yes, our society is
preoccupied with sexuality (whatever that means) and having
sex, but what I mean is that, when we are not thinking about
having sex, we are thinking about gender: who am I as man or
as woman? And who is the other in relation to me?

We have become alarmed at being different because we read
difference in terms of power. We cannot think about each
other without asking, "Who is superior? Who is in charge?" (Of
course, there are both conservative and radical versions of this.)
We cannot think about what it means to be a man or a woman
without immediately thinking about what role each plays, what
tasks each has, what authority each possesses, and what order
exists between him and her. And so sex has disintegrated: we
have forgotten how we complement one another.

These questions are not completely irrelevant, of course. But is
power (with, perhaps, some sex on the side) all that men and
women have to talk about? Don't we have more in common
with each other?

French feminist Luce Irigaray says that "Sexual difference is one of the major philosophical issues, if not the issue, of our age".[27] She is an interesting thinker: she sees sexual difference as a real opportunity for human beings to experience joy, if only we can learn together what it means.

What we need to rediscover is wonder—the gasp of joy that came from the man when he met the woman for the first time and saw himself in her reflected. But we also need to rediscover more than that: we need to rediscover what the man felt when he looked at the woman and saw something quite familiar but also quite foreign. There, they were naked together and were not ashamed. What could that have been like?

HELP

"It is not good that the man should be alone …" (Gen 2:18)

I want to focus now on the way the Bible tells the story of the creation of the first woman—not because my focus is on woman to the exclusion of man, but because it is in these scenes that we see man and woman first meeting each other.

Genesis 2:18 is God's call, and it's kind of strange, given that he has just declared the whole creation "very good" (Gen 1:31). Apparently the man's isolation isn't good for the man, it isn't good for the world and it isn't good as far as God is concerned either. The man is incomplete. He needs 'help'—or, more precisely, a "helper" (v. 18).

Now, we need to be careful here: we tend to cringe at the word 'helper'—as if it implies some kind of personal assistant or maid. But the word 'helper' is used in the Bible of God himself (e.g. Exod 18:4, Deut 33:29 and Ps 54:4)! So there is no implication of inferiority: the woman is the man's co-worker—

his partner—his counterpart.

However, the woman and the man do not exist as individuals for their own sakes with no reference to one another. The word 'helper' reminds us of their need for one another. The making of the woman opens up Adam to the world: it helps him (as he helps her) to be part of the world—to answer the call of God, to carry out his task, to better be himself. The making of the woman is a challenge to the man not to shrink back into himself.

A GENTLE RIBBING

"This at last is bone of my bones ..." (Gen 2:23)

When Adam meets his wife the first time, he immediately recognizes himself. He recognizes the sameness of her; she is not like the animals. Though animals are made from the earth too, they are different—too different. Not so the woman: she is the same as him. She's made of the same stuff.

She is not from a different planet—for example, Venus, or some other celestial body. Self-help books and ancient mythologies say things like that, and the book of Genesis contradicts them both. Adam can see just by looking at her. Here at last is someone who can look him in the eye as his equal—as his counterpart.

God makes her from his rib. This tells us that they are of the same substance. Notably, she comes, not from his head or from his foot, but from his side. She is made from his side because they will stand side by side—two as one.

It is important for us not to forget that men and women are together human first and sexually different second. Our unity is far more shocking than our distinctions.

> And the man and his wife were both naked and were not
> ashamed. (Gen 2:25)

Do you ever watch those shows that shame people because of
their oversized or unattractive bodies? The presenters check the
participants' poo samples, and show them what they eat and
therefore why their body is gross. It's so embarrassing for the
poor people who appear on these shows.

That's shame all right: shame is wanting to hide your hide. And
we particularly attach shame (which is connected to guilt, of
course) to the sexual aspects of our bodies.

Now, I don't think that what the Bible is saying here is some
great argument for nudism. It's not that that's the way things
were meant to be, so we should all just get over it and walk
around with our togs off. No, the nakedness of the husband
and wife is more than their physical state of being unclothed.
They were vulnerable to one another, but still safe. They
were not at risk of being abused or becoming the victim of
selfish lust. They were not laughed at in the weakness of their
flesh, but instead they were delighted in. They needed no
adornment or enhancement to be the man and the woman they
were meant to be. Not an implant or a little blue pill can be
seen. Instead, between them, there is only an uncomplicated
innocence. And nothing else.

OF FROGS AND SNAILS

You might remember this really dumb nursery rhyme:

> What are little boys made of, made of?
> What are little boys made of?

Frogs and snails, and puppy-dogs' tails,
That's what little boys are made of.

What are little girls made of, made of?
What are little girls made of?
Sugar and spice, and all things nice,
That's what little girls are made of.

I used to hate this poem when I was a kid—not because it says there is a difference between boys and girls (no, I was happy for that!) but because it makes the difference a matter of moral superiority of the female over the male. (My sister was very smug about it ...)

What does it mean to be a man or a woman? What I have been trying to say so far is that to be a man or a woman is first and foremost a matter of being human, not something else. It means being part of a race with the other one in it. So it is impossible to ask about manhood or womanhood in isolation, as if they make sense on their own terms.

However, the question about what it means to be a man or a woman is about what we call 'masculinity' and 'femininity'. These words describe roughly not the bits on our bodies so much as the way males and females express their sex in different ways. We use the word 'gender' to describe this.

This is a hard subject to discuss because we tend to focus on fringe examples—people who cross or bend gender in various ways—people who publicly gain lots of attention, perhaps by playing with the 'rules' and conventions we normally accept about the way men and women act in society. It is also a difficult topic because we tend to hear descriptions or observations of masculinity and feminity as prescriptions or ideals. If someone says, "This is what a man is", we immediately think of examples of men who are not like this, or who do not meet this standard in some way.

I think we should just calm down. Here are two reasons why. Firstly, as I was thinking about this, I went for a walk in the town where I live. It is a fairly cosmopolitan city, filled with people from all over the world, so cultural differences are well represented here. I observed a huge variety of people on my walk—people of all sorts of shapes and sizes and races—and it was bleedingly obvious who was a man and who was a woman. Almost all of us are unembarrassed by our gender, and we feel free to express it in a variety of ways: hairstyle, clothes, bodily gestures, actions, even perfumes. Though there are lots of ways of showing it, women are feminine and men are masculine. Gender-bending is the exception, and we know it when we see it.

Secondly, what I observed is actually reflected by the lack of detail you get in the Bible itself. Though the Bible expresses that there is a difference between the genders, it doesn't tell us a great deal about how this should be worked out in practice. It certainly describes masculine and feminine, and it does so in quite an erotic way! But as for rules about who should do the washing up ... well, there just isn't that kind of stuff in it.

What we do see is that there is a bodily difference between man and woman. It's a constant—something they are given to live life with. There are widely acknowledged general differences in physical, chemical and mental patterns. Culture then receives and realizes these differences, expressing them in traditions and customs and practices of daily living, dressing, courtship and family life.

THIS IS MY LOVER

The Song of Songs is a curious Old Testament book. It's a pretty vivid erotic poem in which two lovers speak of their aching desire for one another. It is interesting to note the differences in the way they talk about what excites them about the other. Here's the man:

> How beautiful are your feet in sandals,
>   O noble daughter!
> Your rounded thighs are like jewels,
>   the work of a master hand.
> Your navel is a rounded bowl
>   that never lacks mixed wine.
> Your belly is a heap of wheat,
>   encircled with lilies.
> Your two breasts are like two fawns,
>   twins of a gazelle.
> Your neck is like an ivory tower.
> Your eyes are pools in Heshbon,
>   by the gate of Bath-rabbim.
> Your nose is like a tower of Lebanon,
>   which looks toward Damascus.
> Your head crowns you like Carmel,
>   and your flowing locks are like purple;
>   a king is held captive in the tresses. (Song 7:1-5)

Notice how his eye is caught by her radiance: he is entranced by her. He tells her about her beauty. It is quite clear that it's a feminine body he is praising, with breasts and her long hair featuring high on the list. And he takes time and care and respect in describing her: he doesn't do it in a cheap or pornographic way, as if she had been made just for his use.

But perhaps we are too used to males being fascinated by the physical presence of females. What is surprising for such an old text is the fact that the woman is given a chance to dwell on the way in which the man's body fascinates her:

> My beloved is radiant and ruddy,
>> distinguished among ten thousand.
> His head is the finest gold;
>> his locks are wavy,
>> black as a raven.
> His eyes are like doves
>> beside streams of water,
> bathed in milk,
>> sitting beside a full pool.
> His cheeks are like beds of spices,
>> mounds of sweet-smelling herbs.
> His lips are lilies,
>> dripping liquid myrrh.
> His arms are rods of gold,
>> set with jewels.
> His body is polished ivory,
>> bedecked with sapphires.
> His legs are alabaster columns,
>> set on bases of gold.
> His appearance is like Lebanon,
>> choice as the cedars.
> His mouth is most sweet,
>> and he is altogether desirable.
> This is my beloved and this is my friend,
>> O daughters of Jerusalem. (Song 5:10-16)

The woman is depicted bragging about her man to her friends. But she too is no less delighted by his masculine traits than he is by her feminine ones. Take his strong legs and arms, for example.

Now, culturally, things have changed: we probably don't describe our delight in the other gender in the same way as this. Few of us have ever seen Mount Carmel and even fewer would think to compare that mountain to a person's head, for example. But nonetheless, we do delight in each other. At least, we should.

HERE COMES THE BRIDE

I haven't tried to give a comprehensive account of this topic. To do that, people have written whole books! But I have one last thing to say, and it comes from a passage in the New Testament—from Paul's letter to the Ephesians:

> ... submitting to one another out of reverence for Christ.
> Wives, submit to your own husbands, as to the Lord. For the husband is the head of the wife even as Christ is the head of the church, his body, and is himself its Savior. Now as the church submits to Christ, so also wives should submit in everything to their husbands.
> Husbands, love your wives, as Christ loved the church and gave himself up for her, that he might sanctify her, having cleansed her by the washing of water with the word, so that he might present the church to himself in splendor, without spot or wrinkle or any such thing, that she might be holy and without blemish. (Eph 5:21-27)

The marriage of man and woman is meant, as Paul explains it, to act as a sign—a sign of what Jesus Christ did for his people, the church, by dying on the cross for them. The wife in her submission to her husband (to whom has been given the role of 'head') is modelling the way in which God's people accept from Christ the forgiveness and cleansing they need. The husband, for his part, is to live out his role as head in the marriage—not in assertiveness or domination by the strength of his right arm, but by love. His model is Christ—Christ who laid down his life with the goal of making his people holy and spotless, radiant and blameless. The husband is to treat his wife as he would his own body, using exactly the same tender care he would normally reserve for his own physical being.

Of course, we tend to slip back into thinking about power again when we hear these verses. We want to know who is in charge. But that rather misses the point of the challenge that both woman and man receive here: they must love 'til it hurts, and let themselves be the object of that love. (Sometimes it is harder accepting the love of someone else than being the one who loves ...)

In this way, a man and a woman in the adventure of their marriage have the opportunity of being an image to the world of the future meaning of masculine and feminine. The Bible portrays Jesus as a bridegroom and the church as bride, beautifully dressed for her wedding. What is the dressing of a bride meant to represent? At every wedding I have ever been to, the bride has always been the centre of attention. Her husband does not outshine her on this day. Her clothes are meant to make her utterly glorious. In addition, brides traditionally wear white to symbolize their innocence and purity.

The book of Revelation uses these kinds of ideas to describe the coming together of Christ and his church on the last day:

> And I saw the holy city, new Jerusalem, coming down out of heaven from God, prepared as a bride adorned for her husband. And I heard a loud voice from the throne saying, "Behold, the dwelling place of God is with man. He will dwell with them, and they will be his people, and God himself will be with them as their God." (Rev 21:2-3)

This passage doesn't give us a set of instructions about what we ought to do as men or women. But it shows us something else:

it shows us that male and female are part of God's great plan for the world and for human beings. Indeed, it has always been so.

13 COMMENTS

Joanna It's strange, isn't it, that, in many ways, the world wants to iron out the differences between the genders because difference is a threat. (I can see this tendency in my own thinking as well.) But at other times, we want to highlight the differences.

Bec I don't think that we can separate our gender/sexuality from who we are (not that I think you are saying that). I think you are right—we *do* need to think about who we are in relation to one another—but ultimately this boils down to who we are in Christ. We are who we are in Christ.

Which leads me to wonder how we can rediscover the wonder of when man met woman for the first time with this in mind. If we are seeking to rediscover that bare nakedness (not just in the physical but also in the emotional), does this imply something more than the brother-sister relationship that we see taught in the New Testament?

Mandy I like to use the idea of 'ally' to translate 'helper'. While it has negative overtones of war, it helps to convey the idea of reliance and interdependence of the man and the woman.

Simon I once heard a wedding sermon which basically said that the couple getting married were becoming truly human. It was one of the most embarrassing sermons I have ever heard—embarrassing for all of the truly human single people listening to it.

Michael I cringe with you, Simon. Was Jesus truly human, then? We must remember that the single person is no less a gendered person than the married one.

Bec

"We also need to rediscover more than that: we need to rediscover what the man felt when he looked at the woman and saw something quite familiar but also quite foreign ... It is important for us not to forget that men and women are together human first and sexually different second."

It seems to me that men and women need to learn to make space for one another, rather than demanding that the other conform to their shape. But this makes me wonder about convents and monasteries. If man and woman were created to live in community with both genders and it is far easier to live with and love a member of the same sex, then is living in a convent/monastery a form of escapism? In secluding themselves from the opposite sex/gender in their communities, do they lose something of what it actually means to live in community/relationships the way that God has created us?

Michael

Well, yes! Perhaps you could say the same of single-sex schools, too. I went to a single-sex school and it felt incompletely human to me!

A friend of mine once took Year 8 from the boys' school he was working in to a camp. The campsite director said to him, "You know, last week we had a group of Year 8 girls. And you know, they really are different. All Year 8 girls ever talk about is boys. But boys—all Year 8 boys ever talk about is farts." To me, this pretty much sums up the tragedy of the world!

For a long time, we have tried to protect women and girls by segregation. Feminism even argued for the necessity of 'women's space'—a place where women can flourish and grow unhindered. But I don't think it works. It just gives men license to ignore women.

Maleness and femaleness are a gift to the whole human community, not just to the married ...

Sophie

Clearly much of the authority/superiority complex that we identify with the 'battle of the sexes' is because of the abuse of power by patriarchy throughout history. But I think it is terribly sad that the consequence of acknowledging this abuse of power is a gender-obsessed world. Feminism was and is a political and social movement responding to the breakdown of relationships between men and women across history. All women—particularly feminists—are guilty of navel-gazing—focusing so much on the self and empowerment that we forget to see that this relationship breakdown is a symptom of something bigger. We must stop obsessing about gender, defining ourselves only by 'the other'.

I agree with you, Michael, that it would be more helpful to swing the pendulum the other way and focus on our similarities—most importantly, our relationship to our Creator.

Joanna I think it is really interesting that, as you pointed out in your story about wandering around your town, we can forget many things about a person we've just met—their name, their hair colour, what we were talking about—but the salient point that seems to stay permanently in our head is their sex.

Byron Because gender is woven so deeply into our language (and therefore our thought), it makes gender-bending stand out more because it so obviously causes confusion in a way and at a level that other transgressions of social norms rarely achieve.

Michael You know, I think perhaps our gender is like being given a musical instrument to play: you have to play that instrument, but you have all the freedom and styles that you can express with it. You can even make it sound a bit like another instrument at times. You need to learn the instrument, practise it, make mistakes and get better at it.

Another analogy: gender is a particular language we learn to speak—a language with its own patterns, its own inner grammar ...

Joanna   The 'plane' of gender—the 'spectrum' that is now being taken
          hold of by most academics is actually the strongest threat to
          the biblical understanding of male and female. Though we may
          argue about who is supposed to do what or "who is in charge",
          Christians usually still do this in the context of a world with
          only two genders—two sexes. I think you're right, Michael: this
          was part of the picture all along.

          It is testament to God's great glory and power that he can
          make creatures that are so different and yet so similar, and
          fashion them to be in perfect relationship with himself and
          one another.

Michael   Yes, though I do feel that academics of gender do not operate
          in the 'real' world. Which is to say, starting with our limitless
          freedom, they see the possibilities for free expression within
          each gender as a sign of our radical independence from social
          definitions. The answer isn't to codify what men and women
          can and can't do/wear/be more strongly, but to understand
          properly what gender is: a gift to us people to receive, realize
          and enjoy.

dreams

TO DREAM

Is it too strong a statement to say that, along with our memories, our dreams are what make us human? Our (I would say) God-given capacity to want, desire, imagine, aspire to and hope for a better arrangement of the world sets us apart from the beasts and machines. Do fish dream of speedboats? Did dogs think of canned dog food? Do computers imagine life with more RAM or a larger monitor? Do trees aspire to grow legs or wheels? Do androids dream about having dreams?

Our dreams keep us going. Our dreams keep us motivated—longing—acting on the present to become something in the future. They are our momentum. To be without dreams is like sitting on a bicycle without pedalling: you fall over. When we lose the ability to dream, we become little better than animals, responding to stimuli by instinct, going by nothing more than gut feeling, governed by no more than the chemistry of our bodies and our base drives: hunger, thirst, sex and power. When we lose the ability to dream, we despair and self-destruct.

We also live in line with our dreams. As humans, we can delay gratification in the present in order to achieve a dream. We understand that if we endure present hardship and hard work, we can achieve great things later: advanced prosperity, the end of suffering, personal achievement. In one sense, education tests our ability to dream: if we are continually distracted by our present, we will not achieve as well. However, it is those who dream who achieve.

The human ability to dream is, perhaps, our greatest asset. Think of all we have achieved through dreaming—all the art, music and literature in the world—all the inventions, explorations and achievements of science: all of these rely on our capacity to imagine a world different from the one we are now in. Let's not hold back here: we are truly amazing in our creativity.

US President Woodrow Wilson is said to have once said:

> We grow great by dreams. All big men are dreamers. They see things in the soft haze of a spring day or in the red fire of a long winter's evening. Some of us let these great dreams die, but others nourish and protect them; nurse them through bad days till they bring them to the sunshine and the light which comes always to those who sincerely hope that their dreams will come true ...

I HAVE A DREAM ...

So what do we dream about? Well, for each person, the answer is slightly different. But it is possible to generalize. Usually human dreams concern ourselves and those around us. We may dream of wealth, honour, love, success or some thrilling experience. Did you ever have to write one of those stories in school where you were the main character—the hero? When I was teaching English literature to 13-year-old boys, they would write those stories over and over again—stories like this:

After I scored the winning try for Australia at the football stadium, I went off to the hospital to perform life-saving surgery on the patient that was waiting for me. Then it was home to my blonde wife and our two lovely children in our massive harbourside house with a yacht and two BMWs. I took a call from the Prime Minister who offered me an Order of Australia Medal and a place in his government, but I turned him down.

Our adult dreams are often no more sophisticated than this. We speak of our dream home, our dream holiday, our dream date and our dream lover. Shopping is a form of dreaming. The purpose of advertising is to make us dream that life would be better with the product they're selling. Do you have these dreams?

The other sort of dreams that people have work on a grander scale. They are the great visions of our world—the dreams that affect us all. Communism was a type of dream; Nazism was another. These dreams envisage a utopia—a kind of heaven on earth. One great dreamer was Martin Luther King Jr who said, "I have a dream that one day this nation will rise up and live out the true meaning of its creed: 'We hold these truths to be self-evident: that all men are created equal'".[28] We may dream of gender equality or racial harmony or world peace or the eradication of disease. But our dreams—big or small—are lived out under frustrating conditions.

CASTLES MADE OF SAND

The expectation for our dreams is that, usually, they will not be fulfilled. One of the great tragedies of being human is that we have the ability to dream, but not the ability to achieve all that we dream. We can see the amazing possibilities of this world, but we cannot make them a reality. We know how good it could be, but we don't know why it never is. It is normal for our dreams to be frustrated—normal for our struggle to achieve personal peace, fulfilment, satisfaction, a better world and an end to suffering to remain a struggle. We lack the talent, the drive, the advice, the resources, the luck and the time. Something always frustrates us. We are left trusting our dreams to dumb luck.

1960s rock genius Jimi Hendrix once wrote a very moving song called 'Castles Made of Sand'. It's a song that tells stories:

> As she slams the door in his drunken face,
> And now he stands outside,
> And all the neighbours start to gossip and drool,
> He cries, "Oh, girl, you must be mad,
> What happened to the sweet love you and me had?"
> Against the door, he leans and starts a scene,
> And his tears fall and burn the garden green.
>
> And so castles made of sand fall in the sea, eventually.[29]

'Eventually' was sooner rather than later for Jimi: he choked on his own vomit and died in bed in a London basement flat, aged 27.

But sometimes our dreams *are* realized. We win the lottery, our cheque comes in, we find a soul mate, or we achieve social justice or the end of racist laws. Sometimes all we dream comes to pass because our dreams are modest.

The trouble is that when we achieve our dreams, they are never quite what we wanted in the first place. They never quite fulfil our expectations. Or they are achieved in a fragmentary way. Why is it that rich and successful people are so often miserable? For example, why is that Michael Hutchence, who was rich, successful, sexy, the lead singer of INXS and in the prime of his life, died the way he did in 1997?

In 1985, Bob Geldof famously organized the original Live Aid concert, which was, back then, the biggest concert experience of all time. Held simultaneously on two continents in two stadiums, and broadcast live to millions around the world, all the most famous bands of the day played. At the end of it all at the Wembley concert, Geldof overheard two fans talking. One said to the other, "Is that it?" (Geldof later used this as the title of his autobiography.)

That about sums it up: we can have the best and we can achieve our dreams, and yet we are left saying, "Is that it?" When you achieve what you want, you realize that that wasn't what you wanted. Our dreams are castles made of sand, and the wanting is often better than the having.

BEING THERE

How do we respond to the frustration of our dreams? How can we cope with the disappointment of not getting what we want? How can we avoid despair?

One alternative is to detach from our dreams. This is the Buddhist response and the response of some western philosophies too. If you don't dream, you won't be crushed by the disappointment of your dreams.

Another alternative is to seek escape. It is no accident that the entertainment industry is so huge in our world: it sells us dreams—it helps us escape into a world where dreams do come true, even if it's just for a while. Stephen Spielberg called his company 'Dreamworks', after all. If we can't have a fulfilling relationship, we can, at least, watch someone else pretend to have one. If we can't have a lot of money, we can, at least, watch someone else having it. If we can't have great sex or a terrific body, we can, at least, watch someone else pretending to have it. If we can't be happy, we can, at least, enjoy someone else pretending to be happy.

Strangely, the Bible suggests that it is God who frustrates our dreams. In Romans 8:20, we read that "the creation was subjected to futility, not willingly, but because of him who subjected it, in hope". That is, God has bound this world in frustration, imperfection and decay. Frustration is the very condition of the world in which we live.

But why? Why would the God who made the world do such a thing? Why would he allow us to dream but not allow us the relief of having our dreams fulfilled?

The first reason is that the frustration of our dreams is a wake-up call. When we sense the gap between what we want and what we get, we hear God telling us that there is something more—that this world is *not* all there is—that we were made for something better than this.

The second is that God wants us to know that our dreams are misdirected. Our dreams are second best. When we pursue our dreams in this world, we are pursuing castles made of sand. We are grasping at straws. We don't dream from the source of all dreams. This world is only a shadow of things to come. If we seek our dreams here, we will not find them, or we will find them only in part.

Whatever your dreams, the dream that God has for you and for our world is so much bigger. What we dream is often good because we tend to dream parts of God's dream. Martin Luther King Jr's dream, for example, was a biblical picture of racial harmony and equality, and he used biblical language to express it. But we could have so much more—the whole rather than the part. Right now, we are like people watching an event on TV instead of actually being there.

THE DREAM OF GOD

What God is calling you to do is to share in his dream—to dream God's dream with him. But what is his dream?

We get a glimpse of what God has planned for the universe in the book of Revelation:

> Then I saw a new heaven and a new earth, for the first heaven and the first earth had passed away, and the sea was no more. And I saw the holy city, new Jerusalem, coming down out of heaven from God, prepared as a bride adorned for her husband. And I heard a loud voice from the throne saying, "Behold, the dwelling place of God is with man. He will dwell with them, and they will be his people, and God himself will be with them as their God. He will wipe away every tear from their eyes, and death shall be no more, neither shall there be mourning, nor crying, nor pain anymore, for the former things have passed away."
>
> And he who was seated on the throne said, "Behold, I am making all things new." Also he said, "Write this down, for these words are trustworthy and true." And he said to me, "It is done! I am the Alpha and the Omega, the beginning and the end. To the thirsty I will give from the spring of the water of life without payment." (Rev 21:1-6)

What is so good about this? Well, firstly, God is there. In this new heaven and earth, God is present, and his presence is obvious to everyone. People have an open relationship with him.

Secondly, the city is purified. This new city is dressed like a bride for her husband. She comes from God as a symbol of purity, cleansed from any wrong.

Thirdly, suffering has ended. No more will there be suffering or mourning or pain. That was the old order of things. In this new order, suffering does not exist.

Fourthly, evil is excluded. Those who continue to practise anti-God behaviour (i.e. those rebels who haven't turned to God and received forgiveness) are excluded from this picture.

What's more (and fifthly), the thirsty drink. Thirst is a picture of wanting—of desiring—of longing—of dreaming. To the one who is thirsty, God will give "from the spring of the water of life without payment" (Rev 21:6). It's water that truly satisfies.

God's dream is not somewhere over the rainbow, way up high. It is a vision of what will take place. How is it possible? It's possible because of the Lamb, the husband of the city-bride. The Lamb is, of course, Jesus Christ. Why is he called a Lamb? Because of what he did to bring about God's dream: he acted like a sacrificial lamb, shedding his own blood so that human beings might be purified from all that corrupts them. By dying the death that we should have died, Jesus makes possible the end of suffering, the defeat of all that is evil, satisfaction for the thirsty and the filling of the hungry.

God has already acted on his dream. He did it on the cross when Jesus cleared the mess blocking the road between us and God.

DREAMING WITH GOD

A Christian is one who dreams God's dreams—or seeks to dream God's dreams. Jesus once said "seek first the kingdom of God and his righteousness, and all these things will be added to you" (Matt 6:33). In other words, lay aside your dreams and dream with God—seek to work out his dream for his world in your life. Then, sure enough, all the things you yourself dream will be given to you. The only certain way to achieve what you really dream is to dream what God dreams, hope for what God hopes for, long for what God longs for, and trust not in dumb luck, but in the work of the mighty God himself.

Christians try to pencil in God's dream in the world today. The dream they have isn't a way of avoiding the world, but rather of embracing it—preparing it for what it will one day be. What they do isn't just daydreaming; they try to change the world and shape it according to what God intends for it in the future—by loving God and one another, and by calling on others to do the same.

God has a dream that one day men and women of all races will sit down together at the table of fellowship with him in his name. God has a dream that one day peace will reign, war will end, disease will be eradicated and nation will no longer rise up against nation. God has a dream that one day you will stand before him cleansed of all your sin. God has a dream that one day you'll be the person he intended you to be.

Won't you dream with him?

5 COMMENTS

Sam	Are dreams also a reflection of the "eternity into man's heart" thing (Eccl 3:11), giving us a sense that we were made for better things?
Byron	Many of our dreams, when fulfilled, turn out to be not

simply disappointing, they're actually nightmares. Take the Lotto winner who discovers that the money destroys her relationships, the corporate ladder climber whose workaholism destroys his health, the politician whose reforms lead to the establishment of new forms of slavery.

Michael "Be careful what you wish for", etc. Yes, I guess I'm trying to say that our imaginations, which liberate us in so many ways, are not imaginative enough—or that we mis-imagine what it will be like to live with our dreams.

Also, we are so conditioned to longing that having what we long for can be quite disturbing. Some of us never adjust to it.

Marty Sorry to put a negative spin on things, but it seems that an obvious source of frustration for our dream isn't that we dream for too little but that we dream for too much—things which are unrealistic. Maybe there is wisdom in being content with second best. I don't think this is a cop-out. I think it's striving to dream in harmony with reality—especially a reality which sees the fulfilment of dreams coming at the end. This is why some churches have had such a high drop-out rate: they promise too much *now*. I'm beginning to feel ripped off because society has taught me to reject the art of contentment. We are told never to be content with what we have, and this in turn leads to frustration. Reconstructing this expectation is hard to do. I'm not sure how you do it but I'm starting to feel that it's something I need to do.

It seems to me that we want to focus our dreams on God's future, but what we need to do is deal with what that means for our desires in the present age in an earthy and honest manner. I still have 50 years left (God-willing) to deal with all this. I'd prefer not to have these years ruined by unrealistic dreams.

▶ *"God wants us to know that our dreams are misdirected."*

What about unfulfilled Christian desires? Are they "second best"?

Michael   Well, Marty, I figure that part of being a Christian is having a thoroughly revamped imagination.

                We shouldn't be too content with how things are anyway because we'll start to forget that life isn't yet what it could be. So we are called to be content in the midst of yearnings (Phil 4:11-13).

deep trouble

THE EVIL NEXT DOOR

We've been talking a lot about You and what it means to be You. And I'm sorry to have to be so blunt, but it's obvious to everyone who knows you: something is deeply wrong with you.

But you aren't alone. If you are a human being (and if any non-human beings are reading this book, could you please let me know?), then not all is well. In every aspect of humanity, there are deficiencies, errors and stains. These are not just innocent mistakes; they are actions worthy of blame.

I don't think I am being a doom and gloom merchant here. History, economics, art, linguistics, literature and politics should all tell us that the human tendency to warp everything is pretty strong. It's like King Midas in reverse: everything we touch turns to lead. And it is the moments of our greatest triumphs that become the scenes of our greatest evils. Haven't you noticed?

Dr Harold Shipman was a fairly ordinary-looking man who was well respected as a GP in northern England. His patients—mainly older women—spoke very fondly of him. Only it turned out that, over a period of some years, he had been bumping them off. He would typically visit a patient and quietly administer her a lethal dose of diamorphine. He was then able to sign the death certificate and recommend against an autopsy. He remained undetected for years. Finally, Shipman was charged and convicted of the murders of 15 of his patients. It is thought that he may have killed as many as 200 more.

Why did he do this? Who knows? Shipman refused to comment on his behaviour, and pleaded his innocence. When he finally killed himself in prison in 2004, there were still no explanations for his murderous spree. It was an evil of extraordinary proportions made even more sinister by its suburban ordinariness. Shipman did not even seem that deranged. He apparently just enjoyed wielding the power of life and death over those in his care. You couldn't say he was a sicko, or point to a history of child abuse or an obvious psychiatric disorder. In one sense, his actions were not violent; he just administered a simple, clean injection.

It's this that makes the case all the more terrifying—that an ordinary, educated and well-off human being could do something so appalling while remaining so normal outwardly. It means we can't distance ourselves from Shipman's evil, much as we might like to. This is not the evil of Tolkien's Mordor; it's the evil next door.

MAN HANDS ON MISERY TO MAN

It is not just that some individuals are exceptionally bad. There seems to be a distortion in each human individual. You see it when some disaster hits a city, and law and order breaks down. Wherever you are in the world, looters will move in. And who are they? Oh, just ordinary people. What does this show? It shows that what stops ordinary people from stealing in normal circumstances is not their natural goodness but the fear of getting caught. If someone thinks they can get away with it, they will try it.

It is not just that individuals do bad things; human beings are entangled in vast networks of evil. Take families, for example. Gloomy English poet Philip Larkin once wrote, "Man hands on misery to man".[30] (He certainly had a decent go at handing on misery himself in this particular poem!) Larkin might have been dismal, but he was right. We inherit the faults of our parents and pass them on to our children. This was the great insight of 20th-century psychology.

The Bible's diagnosis matches these observations. When Paul wrote his famous letter to the Romans, he wanted to deliver some good news—good news about salvation in Jesus Christ. But in explaining why this was good news, he had to show why there is also some bad news. So he started by telling them that even though God's character is obvious from the world he has made, people everywhere persist in refusing to get it. You might call it wilful ignorance: "they became futile in their thinking, and their foolish hearts were darkened" (Rom 1:21b).

But that's not all. Humans are still very religious. What they have done is switched worship of the true God with the worship of idols. The 'normal' human choice, according to Paul, is for darkness instead of enlightenment.

This leads to terrible chaos for human beings in the world. Paul describes the debauchery that results from false worship as a desecration of the human body (Rom 1:21-32). Deviant sexual behaviours are intermingled with deviant worship. What Paul is talking about is the complete breakdown of the image of God in men and women.

TWISTED

But this is not the most surprising thing Paul has in store. You might think that what he says cannot be applied to people who had God's law. It is an honour and an advantage to be an Israelite, but in terms of his judgement on sin, God shows no favourites. There is no room for proud boasting on the basis of national superiority or moral achievement. The universality of human rebellion against God does not allow for ethnic exceptions.

Paul gives us what pretty much amounts to a family history of sin. The way we human beings are can be traced back to our ancestors—to the first sin of Adam and Eve. Sin spread out from them like a genetic disease, and the rest of the human race reaped the consequences. However, we are not condemned for something that isn't ours. This is the big point, really: somehow in one of us, all of us sinned. It does no good to claim that Adam was a poor representative for us and that perhaps I could have done better. That's just not the reality of the matter.

What is the result? The result is that it is not just the outer world of our actions that has been affected, but the inner world of our desires and longings. We are the slaves of sin, even on the inside. We are torn between the desire to do good and the fact that we will never live up to this desire. Paul captures the existential paradox of our will perfectly: sin is a force that has humans enslaved, yet the human is still the agent of his own demise. Since Adam and Eve, the human will has become twisted against itself.

VICTIMS AND PERPETRATORS

However, we are not merely the do-ers of sins; we are also its victims. Sin happens to us as much as we engage in it. We are sinking in a bog of our own digging. We need rescuing from the whole realm of sin—a realm we inhabit. We are pathetic creatures.

In other words, sin is not merely a matter of breaking an abstract moral code. It's personal: it's between us and God. It is a false worship—a worship not of the true God, but of a false one. It is worship of the god of the self or the god of the created things around us.

Because of these things, God's judgement hangs over us all, and his judgement is manifested in the fact that we die.

Which is what we need to talk about next ...

6 COMMENTS

Byron   But I haven't killed 200 old women. Am I really the same as Dr Shipman?

Drew   ▶ *"It is not just the outer world of our actions that has been affected, but the inner world of our desires and longings."*

Does this mean I am capable of even deceiving myself that I may be right with God? Can we deceive ourselves into thinking we have faith?

Michael   Byron: I am pleased to hear it! My point is not that we are exactly the same as Dr Shipman but that we aren't exactly different either. We differ from him only by degree.

Drew: Well, I should think so. After all, Jesus said,

> "Not everyone who says to me, 'Lord, Lord,' will enter the kingdom of heaven, but the one who does the will of my Father who is in heaven. On that day many will say to me, 'Lord, Lord, did we not prophesy in your name, and cast out demons in your name, and do many mighty

works in your name?' And then will I declare to them,
'I never knew you; depart from me, you workers of
lawlessness.'" (Matt 7:21-23)

Drew   So what hope do we have that we aren't deceiving ourselves?

Michael   Perhaps the answer lies in the nature of faith itself. Faith, I
           think, is the kind of thing that is hard to deceive yourself about
           since it involves such an acknowledgement of powerlessness
           and a reliance on God's approval of Jesus. In contrast, you can
           deceive yourself into thinking that God approves of you very
           easily. What do you think?

Drew   I was thinking of mental illnesses where our perceptions of the
           world are shaken and many things in which we put our faith
           are threatened. I agree: true faith comes from outside of us.
           But many things masquerade as faith, and sometimes being
           shaken is a good thing because it shows us the true nature of
           faith.

           So I think suffering, faith, self-deception—these things are never
           far from each other. Ironically, perhaps, Jesus' words "I never
           knew you" are, perhaps, scariest for those who have faith ...

death

THE GIFT OF DEATH?

It is common these days for people to say they don't want other people to be sad at their funerals. Instead, they say, "I want everyone to have a party in my memory". This, I think, is a clear denial of the sadness and loneliness of death, and the pain of leaving loved ones behind. The pretence is that death has become acceptable—a natural part of life.

Recently in Britain they conducted a survey of the most popular songs played at funerals. In the top five were Monty Python's 'Always Look on the Bright Side of Life' and 'I Did It My Way' (sung by either Frank Sinatra or Robbie Williams).[31] Doesn't this indicate an attitude of complete denial of the obvious? I feel like saying, "Yes, you did it your way, and look where you've ended up!"—only that kind of thing doesn't go down so well at funerals.

Philosopher Jacques Derrida once wrote, "If I don't reach the place where I can be reconciled with death, then I will have failed. If I have one goal, it is to accept death and dying."[32] Religions clearly won't accept the naturalness of death, so Derrida wants a better way of thinking about death instead of imagining it reversed the way religions do. Since he died in 2004, I have often wondered whether he reached his 'reconciliation with death'.

I think a similar desire for some kind of control is behind the euthanasia movement. Euthanasia, of course, means 'good death'. What its advocates imagine is that a quick and relatively painless assisted suicide is a good way to die—a way that honours the dignity of the life just lived. Somehow, a technologically assisted, clean death is more humanizing than a long painful battle with an ugly disease. The manner of death has some kind of bearing on the meaning and dignity of the person. There's a point to this, actually: if you have ever watched a friend or relative die of an illness, the hardest thing about it is the way in which the disease robs them of the things that make them distinctively them: losing your bodily functions is close to losing your self.

ON THE RUN

I wonder if our delight in murder mysteries and in detailed descriptions from forensic pathologists in shows like *Law & Order, CSI* and all the rest is because we like to feel that every death is explainable. We like to imagine that the causes of death are possible to locate in the world with science and technology. The heroes of these shows are masters of death: they are able to read—even exegete—dead bodies and deliver justice. This is, perhaps, a pointer to our deeper longings for an explanation for what we find so inexplicable: death.

I would like to suggest that our culture is very, very afraid of death. I used to think this wasn't so. For the Victorians, who saw death all around them, death became a morbid obsession. In contrast, most of us are happily spared continual trips to the undertakers.

However, the more I think about it, the more I think death is stalking us more than ever. For example, the modern cult of busyness comes from a deep fear of death. There seems to be less and less time these days. Time is something we now manage, share or flex (but hopefully not 'do'). It is more important to save time than to spend it. It's loathsome to waste it and painful to kill it. Time is money.

We live in the great age of the time-saving device: the microwave, the word processor, the elevator, the dishwasher, the vacuum cleaner, the automobile, the long-haul passenger aircraft, 5GB of RAM. Instant coffee. Fast food. In the 60s, drugs were for escape—for slowing time down. In the 90s and the noughties, the drug of choice is caffeine, the ultimate stimulant. We chase hyper-awareness rather than hallucination. Only our society could have produced a drug called 'speed'. The latest fad is those high-energy high-priced vitamin drinks which are designed to explode you out of that snoozy period after lunch to take control of what's left of your day. Go fast—all the time.

We are chronically impatient. But what are we running from? Death.

But of course, as Emily Dickinson wrote:

> Because I could not stop for Death—
>   He kindly stopped for me—[33]

Death won't wait until you have an opening in your diary.

TO BE, OR ...?

The idea of our non-existence is clearly terrifying. It is nauseating. It weighs heavily on our shoulders. It is crippling to contemplate. When you consider not-being, what do you think about? The sheer loneliness of it haunts me most because it is a loss of love.

Perversely, though, we have also developed a tolerance of suicide. Hamlet is the Shakespearean figure we most identify with: "To be, or not to be, that is the question", he asks himself, wondering whether it is worth going on.[34] The suicidal person believes he has power over the randomness of death and so, in a bizarre way, he may feel he has cheated death. A Year 10 class I discussed this topic with were completely confident that if a person wanted to commit suicide, then it was their choice, and you couldn't go against it if that's what they wanted to do.

The world of the Bible was also a world haunted by death. The pagan mythology of death did nothing to comfort people: Hades was a shadowy horrible place that lay in the destiny of all. For the Jews, it was no different: Sheol, the place of the dead, was not a place of redemption or comfort but rather a shadowy nether land. The signs and symbols of death were nauseating to the people of Israel: they labelled them 'unclean'.

As far as the people Jesus met were concerned, they were under a sentence of death. All around him, Jesus saw the effects of evil and sin. Sickness, disability and death cast a long shadow over the lives of the people. They were browbeaten, exploited, poor and leaderless. They were enslaved to a foreign power and ruled by a corrupt religious hierarchy. Even more serious, it seemed as though Satan himself walked unchained through the land. The Messiah, it had been promised long ago, would be the one through whom the God of all the world would save Israel and the world. How would he do that? By offering himself as a sacrifice—by carrying the judgement that was coming on the world himself.

Mark in his Gospel shows us Jesus walking among the living dead and bringing life. The healing of Simon's mother-in-law, the lepers and the paralytic all restore them to life

(Mark 1:29-2:12). The episode on the Sea of Galilee shows an almost nonchalant Jesus calming the storm in response to the disciples' cry. "Teacher, do you not care that we are perishing?" they said. "Why are you so afraid?" he asked. "Have you still no faith?" (Mark 4:35-40). Later, he met a demoniac who lived among the tombs—a man haunted by death. He was unclean, he was clearly mad and he communed only with the dead. Jesus restored him to sanity and society—to life, in fact—by sending his demons into some pigs who subsequently drowned (Mark 5:1-13). And just after this, Jesus reversed death itself when he encountered Jairus, the desperate father of a 12-year-old girl (Mark 5:21-43).

Despite witnessing all these things, when Jesus came to them walking on water, his disciples thought they had seen a ghost and were terrified (Mark 7:45-52).

HOLLOW DEATH

When Jesus announced to Peter and the other disciples that his destiny was to have an encounter with death—that the Christ was to sacrifice himself on behalf of all Israel—he was met with bewilderment and even anger (Mark 8:31-32). It is his encounter with death that they didn't understand: they still imagined Jesus' kingdom as something won in this world. They pictured it as a victory over the Romans, not a victory over the grave. They didn't see why it required his death. (They certainly didn't foresee their own martyrdoms!)

But the death of Jesus changed everything. Jesus did not avoid his death; instead, he almost seemed to have a death wish. Yet his death was one of utter humiliation. The crowd turned against him, his own religious leaders arranged his trial, the Roman bureaucracy under Pilate failed to uphold justice but succeeded in keeping the peace (temporarily, anyway), and his friends betrayed, denied and deserted him. In the end, his only followers at his cross were a group of downtrodden women. Was there any meaning in the madness?

The centurion, one of the witnesses to Jesus' death, said it best. When he saw how Jesus died, he declared, "Truly this man was the Son of God!" (Mark 15:39). Here on the lips of a rank pagan was the true verdict: this was Israel's Messiah, the King of the Jews, as he said he was. When this pagan man considered the remarkable events he had witnessed, he could see that this was not the meaningless execution of another pathetic Jewish rebel. Something else was going on here on the cross—something on a cosmic scale.

Jesus was buried by his despairing followers (Mark 15:42-47). On the Sunday, his women friends came to put spices on his body. But when they got there, they were gripped by a new fear: the tomb was empty. Their reaction shows that they still misunderstood what had happened (Mark 16). Eventually their terror would be answered by Jesus' reappearance in the flesh. Mark leaves us guessing as to how this was resolved: we have to imagine the tearful reunion and Jesus comforting the women.

Nevertheless, following Jesus' resurrection, the disciples were led into a new life of hope—hope that both sin and death had been defeated and surpassed. Now they had no reason to fear death because the sting of death—namely, sin—had been drawn: death's arrogance in thinking that it had mastery over us had now been proven hollow.

REAL DIGNITY

Not only were Christians now released from their fear of death and its effects through Jesus' resurrection; they could remain in fellowship with the dead. That is to say, the worst effect of death (that is, separation) is not final.

Interestingly, Christian burial practices became quite distinctive: they buried their dead in the catacombs—in the tunnels under the city—and many in Europe adopted the practice of building their churches *in the midst of the tombstones*—in other words, in the centre of what would have been unclean for Israel and terrifying for pagans. In these buildings, Christians met in fellowship with those who had 'fallen asleep'.

That's how Paul told Christians to grieve: to think of those who had died as not permanently separated from them:

> But we do not want you to be uninformed, brothers, about those who are asleep, that you may not grieve as others do who have no hope. For since we believe that Jesus died and rose again, even so, through Jesus, God will bring with him those who have fallen asleep. For this we declare to you by a word from the Lord, that we who are alive, who are left until the coming of the Lord, will not precede those who have fallen asleep. For the Lord himself will descend from heaven with a cry of command, with the voice of an archangel, and with the sound of the trumpet of God. And the dead in Christ will rise first. Then we who are alive, who are left, will be caught up together with them in the clouds to meet the Lord in the air, and so we will always be with the Lord. Therefore encourage one another with these words. (1 Thess 4:13-18)

I once knew two Christians who died of terminal illnesses. They made me wonder whether Christians die differently. I was forced to review the romanticism I had about Christians dying: I had thought that it would be easier—and maybe it is, in some ways. But it is still very, very hard. Ultimately, death is still a fearful and horrible thing. For all the beauty of life—for all the zest and zing of the body—we should not deny that our bodies are in a downward slide. When we die, we will be afraid of the pain and discomfort, terrified of separation, angry at missing out on seeing our loved ones grow and change, and sad for what might have been as all the options of life freeze behind us.

Of the two people I knew who died of terminal illnesses, one was only 33 years old and the mother of two small children. The other was a little older. Both were people of remarkable capacity, dear to those who knew them and occupying the centre of their families' worlds. I didn't see either of them denying the badness of death, or pretending that death could be beaten if you just willed it hard enough (though I'm sure both would have loved to have beaten death more than anything). But I didn't see either person cowed with despair by it. Death since Jesus is not a full stop; it is merely a pause—a semi-colon.[35]

There is real dignity in this kind of death because the person is not going to be dissolved by it. Pain and suffering do not destroy our dignity; if anything ever did that, it was sin. But with those things surpassed, death has only a lease on us; it has never bought us outright.

12 COMMENTS

Anonymous There is something perfectly and appropriately distressing about watching a loved one die. In the face of death, life suddenly becomes humbling, frighteningly and sickeningly stark.

As Christians, we have a huge responsibility to care for those dying and grieving—to love and serve them as Jesus did, to remind them that their identity is not found in their failing body or grief-stricken mind, to tend to their sores and their tears (especially when it is messy and confronting), to share the message of peace found in Jesus.

> *"If you have ever watched a friend or relative die of an illness, the hardest thing about it is the way in which the disease robs them of the things that make them distinctively them."*

Yes, I agree to an extent, but there is also something strangely helpful (in the long run) in seeing someone slowly shut down (from my experience, anyway). The idea of just turning someone 'off' at a convenient moment for all just seems too perfect to be the right thing to do. Sometimes, I think, things are meant to be 'messy' (from our perspective). A product, perhaps, of living in a fallen world? An opportunity to be reminded of God's sovereignty and love, and his hand over all in the face of personal turmoil? A call to trust him in the face of immense struggle?

Bec   Death is a terrible and unnatural thing. It rarely fails to reduce me to tears—whether I know the deceased or not. It's the grief that does it—knowing that it shouldn't be this way. I think an aspect of grief ties in with the fact that we are made in the image of God. And grief serves as a reminder of the enormity of what occurred within the Godhead when God the Son died.

Michael Is death natural or unnatural? From one point of view, it is the most natural thing in the world ...

Byron   > *"Religions clearly won't accept the naturalness of death, so Derrida wants a better way of thinking about death instead of imagining it reversed the way religions do."*

This is a very profound insight. Christianity, at least, envisages not simply the reversal of death, but its overcoming. Paul calls death "the last enemy" (1 Cor 15:26), and though God usually turns enemies into friends through reconciliation, he says that death remains to be 'defeated' through universal resurrection. It is just this protest against death that keeps Christianity from ever being completely reconciled to how things are now. That is why Christianity can never simply be a friend of the status quo. Death is ugly and wrong. There can be great heroism in facing it—there can be times when there are things worse than it—there can be good times despite its approach—but to have reached a place where one is reconciled with death would seem a kind of failure ...

Bec   ▶ *"Is death natural or unnatural?"*

Well, were we created with death in mind? Is death a natural part of life, or is it simply a part of life?

Emma   Along with the 'faster faster faster' approach to life comes anxiety, adrenaline running wild. Humans just aren't built to sustain this kind of pace.

Michael   No, and it kills many of us ...

Benjamin   I've been wrestling with the dichotomy between Jesus' life-giving actions and all his outrageous claims about being God/the source of life/the Messiah/the fulfilment of every powerful sprirtual or physical icon for power and good in everyone's minds. It looks to me like his claims are bigger than his actions. Yes, he walked among the 'living dead', but he only brought life to a few, like the man at the Bethesda pool. He's very secretive and stingy with all that power. Not many get in on life. But his claims are *enormous* and all-encompassing. I find it disturbing. Or, as Megan said the other night, "People live and then die wretched and alone. Please comment."

Michael	Hmm, I wish I knew what to say at this point! The holding back of Jesus is, I could say, because his miracles are not his main task. At this point, he isn't about ruling with power but about dying as a victim/sacrifice. Perhaps the answer is in the temptation story where the devil offers him a chance to display decisively his power and authority (Luke 4:1-13). But it's a shortcut …
Byron	If Jesus was 'holding back' while alive, doesn't this just push the problem forward to our time? Why is he still holding back? Peter suggests that this is due to God's *patience* (2 Pet 3:8-9)—that the nature of the divine cure is so thorough that, unless you're ready for it, it might be the end of you. This is because the problem is not simply that we are *victims* of evil powers beyond our control (though this is also true, and perhaps more true for some), but that we are also *perpetrators* of injustice and suffering in others (in ways big and small— again, some more than others). We need forgiveness as well as rescue. So to be rescued requires the humility of admitting our need and asking for help, and the courage to say "I'm sorry. Help me start again."
Drew	▶ *"Death since Jesus is not a full stop."* Was there dignity in death before Jesus came along—for Jews or anybody else?
Michael	Well, the Jews held up an ideal of dying old and full of years, surrounded by your family and friends, having enjoyed a full and righteous life. But as Ecclesiastes shows, this wasn't really enough—even for the few who were privileged to die this way. It still rendered your earthly life 'vanity', or 'mist' (which is the word *'hebel'* in Hebrew). Death just isn't a satisfactory end to the human story.

what next?

HEAVY MATTER

It's an ancient question: what happens to us when we die? Death is such an unknown to us that it is no wonder that there have been a number of speculations about what comes next. Perhaps we are reincarnated, as the eastern religions say: our spirit leaves our body and goes on to inhabit another body—perhaps not even a human one—just as it has before. Or perhaps our bodies and spirits part ways, and we hang around as ghosts. Or perhaps there's nothing there at all: perhaps, after we die, there is no 'after we die'.

Something very different to any of these options happened to Jesus of Nazareth. His friends believed they saw him, talked with him and even ate with him after he died. And he wasn't what we might call a ghost or a spirit. Neither was he some kind of zombie. He was a full human being raised from the dead. This became the thing they went around trying to explain.

When Paul preached to the philosophers at Athens, they scoffed at the very idea of resurrection of the dead. Likewise it seems that when Paul went down the road to Corinth, he met those who thought the resurrection body distasteful and ridiculous. People asked him, "How are the dead raised? With what kind of body do they come?" (1 Cor 15:35), as if this question would flummox him and expose the silliness of his teaching. Yeah right, Paul. Whatever.

This is no great surprise: in Greco-Roman culture generally, the human body was despised. In the great chain of being, the body was considered to be 'heavy' matter, as opposed to the 'light' matter of the soul. At death, the soul escaped the prison of the body. For example, around the same time as Paul, the philosopher Epictetus wrote:

> For they say, "What am I? A poor, miserable man, with my wretched bit of flesh." Wretched. Indeed; but you possess something better than your "bit of flesh". Why then do you neglect that which is better, and why do you attach yourself to this?[36]

To think that the poor body could be part of a glorious human future was a joke. When Paul went and spoke to the philosophers in Athens, it was the idea of the resurrection that really made some of them gag; they just couldn't accept it as a reasonable idea.

A POSTHUMAN FUTURE?

Sometimes we really feel the need to escape the limits of our bodies. I don't know about you, but often I sense that the human self is capable of so much more than the body allows. The soaring of our spirits is limited by our bodies' decay. We could be so much more if only we weren't bodies. Feminist writer Donna Haraway imagines what she calls a 'posthuman' future where we can escape the banality of the body by becoming cyborgs: half human, half machine.[37] If you have a hearing aid, you are, in fact, already a cyborg. (Tell that to Granny next time you see her ...)

Most people imagine either that the soul escapes the body in death and goes to live on some higher plane—a 'better place'—or that, because there is no soul, the body (which is a product of evolutionary chance) merely dissolves in the grave (so we'd better get used to the idea). Just as in the time of the New Testament, today it seems impossible to imagine a future for the body.

And yet the Bible testifies to God's commitment to his good creation—to mend it and transform it. This includes our bodies. In fact, the human body—in particular, one human body—is the trigger for the change that affects the whole universe. The most startling and, perhaps, the least believed of all the claims of Scripture for our bodies is that we will be resurrected from the dead.

WAITING, WAITING ...

Because of sin, the body is under the sentence of death. But Romans 8:11 says:

> If the Spirit of him who raised Jesus from the dead dwells in you, he who raised Christ Jesus from the dead will also give life to your mortal bodies through his Spirit who dwells in you.

Through sharing the Spirit in the resurrection of Jesus, we can look forward to bodily life as adopted heirs of God. It's all the more reason to "Let not sin therefore reign in your mortal body" (Rom 6:12).

At the moment, the creation, which is in "bondage to corruption" and "subjected to futility" as the Apostle Paul puts it (Rom 8:21, 20), is waiting. What is it waiting for? It's waiting for "the revealing of the sons of God" (Rom 8:19).

What we see as the pains and aches of earthly existence—"the suffering of this present time"—are really the expectant groans of the delivery ward. (Having been in a delivery ward three or four times myself, I reckon they'd be more like 'screams' than 'groans'.) And what do we await—we, the animals, the trees, the hills and the rest of the children of God? The moment of our "adoption as sons, the redemption of our bodies" (Rom 8:23). Just as the sin of Adam sentenced not just human bodies but the whole creation to entropy (which, here, means something like 'steady deterioration'), so the coming to life of the second Adam means the liberation of the whole creation, including human bodies.

AT THE BLAST OF THE TRUMPET

But can we get any more information on what this will look like? Paul's response to the scoffers in 1 Corinthians 15:35-49 is where we now turn:

> But someone will ask, "How are the dead raised? With what kind of body do they come?" You foolish person! What you sow does not come to life unless it dies. And what you sow is not the body that is to be, but a bare kernel, perhaps of wheat or of some other grain. But God gives it a body as he has chosen, and to each kind of seed its own body. For not all flesh is the same, but there is one kind for humans, another for animals, another for birds, and another for fish. There are heavenly bodies and earthly bodies, but the glory of the heavenly is of one kind, and the glory of the earthly is of another. There is one glory of the sun, and another glory of the moon, and another glory of the stars; for star differs from star in glory.
>
> So is it with the resurrection of the dead. What is sown is perishable; what is raised is imperishable. It is sown in

dishonor; it is raised in glory. It is sown in weakness; it is raised in power. It is sown a natural body; it is raised a spiritual body. If there is a natural body, there is also a spiritual body. Thus it is written, "The first man Adam became a living being"; the last Adam became a life-giving spirit. But it is not the spiritual that is first but the natural, and then the spiritual. The first man was from the earth, a man of dust; the second man is from heaven. As was the man of dust, so also are those who are of the dust, and as is the man of heaven, so also are those who are of heaven. Just as we have borne the image of the man of dust, we shall also bear the image of the man of heaven.

God's process of redemption is in keeping with his process of creation. That is the point of the seed analogy: the Creator's power enables the dead seed to bring forth a new plant, which explains how the dead are raised. He does it all the time with seeds; why not with bodies?

Similarly, God has ordered bodies in different ways: the heavenly and earthly bodies differ in glory, for example, but they are still parts of the creation order. So it is with the resurrection body and its relationship to the old earthly body.

The fulfilment and destiny of humanity, having originated from dusty first Adam, now lies in the second Adam who came from heaven (1 Cor 15:45, 47-8). The new race of human beings is now being formed according to the type of the man from heaven: they bear his stamp (v. 49).

When the trumpet sounds, we will leave behind our ordinary, corrupt, decaying flesh-and-blood existence. We will be re-clothed in immortality—with the kind of body Jesus has. This will happen to both those who have died and those who are still alive when he returns.

The new humanity will not shuffle off in its slippers to live in a place called 'heaven' which is not that different from a retirement home. Instead, the change will come from where Jesus is right now—in his own risen and life-giving body. It will completely change our dusty bodies. Paul says "Your life is hidden with Christ in God", but it will one day be revealed in glory when Christ appears (Col 3:3-4).

But Paul does not just call our attention to the hope of the resurrection. On account of the resurrection, he actually directs our gaze to the present time: "Therefore, my beloved brothers, be steadfast, immovable, always abounding in the work of the Lord, knowing that in the Lord your labor is not in vain" (1 Cor 15:58). Your faith is not in vain. In the words of those American theologians the Red Hot Chili Peppers, "This life is more than just a read-through".[38] What we do with and to our bodies now lasts into the future of God.

ECHOES IN ETERNITY

The work of our hands has been rescued from futility. We have no grounds to say, along with most Aussies, 'eat, drink and be merry for tomorrow we die'. Instead, we need to come to a sober and right mind, and sin no more. In fact, the reason a Christian must choose right over wrong is underpinned by the resurrection: the whole point of keeping your body from sexual immorality is that it will be raised. The whole point of keeping order with the other members of the body of Christ is that you share together a resurrected reality. The whole point of not giving yourself over to your appetites is that your body is made, not for food, but for the resurrected Lord. Paul says:

> Let not sin therefore reign in your mortal body, to make you obey its passions. Do not present your members

to sin as instruments for unrighteousness, but present yourselves to God as those who have been brought from death to life, and your members to God as instruments for righteousness. (Rom 6:12-13)

"Instruments of righteousness": I like that.

Russell Crowe, one of the most influential philosophers of our time, once said, in the guise of General Maximus, the disciple of Marcus Aurelius the Stoic Emperor, "What we do in life echoes in eternity".[39] He is right of course, but neither the ancient writers nor our contemporaries have any coherent reason to believe it. The Christian hope in the resurrection body actually explains it, avoiding the pitfalls and charting a middle course between hatred of the body and worship of the body. The difference, too, is that Christian hope is anchored in the historical event of Jesus' rising from the dead.

For this reason, we can hazard more than a good guess about the future of the body. We have a visible example.

5 COMMENTS

Byron	This 'heavy matter' idea hung round for a while. The fourth/fifth-century bishop Augustine of Hippo (I don't think that name was quite as ridiculous in his day) had to keep explaining to his contemporaries how it was that Jesus could still have a body and yet be with his Father who (as we all know) 'art in heaven'. It was a serious question for them: they wanted to know why he wouldn't fall down again!
Drew	Is the resurrection 'posthuman' in other ways?
Michael	Hmm. 'Posthuman': well, I am not happy that the resurrection is posthuman. It's more neo-human—more intensely and

gloriously human than ever before.

Mandy   Could the need to escape the limits of our bodies have
        something to do with the frailty that we see in our bodies
        now? Our bodies change so much from birth to old age. Some
        of the changes are welcome as we reach maturity and greater
        strength from being a child to being an adult. But some are
        unwelcome: our eyesight begins to fail and our muscles waste
        away.

Byron   If Paul is right in Romans 8, then when we're having a really
        hard time and feeling so frustrated that we can't even find
        the words, we are in touch with reality. This is what the whole
        created order is doing. Furthermore, this expectant longing—
        this yearning for liberation from bondage to decay—is not only
        properly 'worldly', it is also 'spiritual', since God's Holy Spirit
        also expresses "groanings too deep for words" (Rom 8:26).

        Therefore, to be truly 'Spirit'-ual—to be a follower of Jesus—to
        be Christian—doesn't mean you've got it all together—that you
        feel on top of the world all the time.

the real You

THE HUMAN BEING: A GUIDE FOR THE PERPLEXED

You may have found this whole process frustrating. We have been trying to discover who You are—what a human being is—to have a good look at ourselves in the mirror, if you like. But although we have certainly caught glimpses in these pages, I think in many ways the mystery has only become deeper.

It is hard to make sense of us because we are so complex. We are paradoxical beings—glorious, on the one hand, yet grotesque, on the other. Just when something about us starts to come into focus, it seems to go blurry again. In one sense, that has been the message of this book—that human beings can't just grasp their own true meaning immediately, even if it feels like it's just around the corner.

It seems that we can't understand ourselves without some help. I said a long time ago that Jesus lived one of the great human lives. People pretty much agree with this, even though they may disagree as to what the significance of this life was. Christianity goes further and makes the claim that Jesus' life was the ultimate human life—human life the way it ought to be lived. A great theologian once said "this man is man".[40]

Now, having said that, we need to be careful. This doesn't mean that we can just paint Jesus in colours that suit us. There are plenty of laughable pictures around of Jesus with blond hair and European features to warn us of the danger of going that way. When we say that Jesus is what a human being ought to be, we aren't saying that he could be like any human being. He was one human being in particular—a man of his time and place. He didn't contain all of humanity in him, and he is not a blank canvas inviting us to paint him as we wish.

It is better to think of him as the measure of all human life. His life is the yardstick, as far as being a human goes.

A RISKY BUSINESS

Does your family have a skeleton in the closet—some piece of information that casts members of the family in a less than glorious light? People who are into family histories are always finding these juicy pieces of information that their grandparents declined to pass on. (No doubt they hoped instead that these things would somehow disappear in the mists of time.) For example, I discovered that my step-great-grandfather was shot dead on Eddy Ave, Sydney (which is not a nice part of town, even today). It was just after he went to the races one Saturday afternoon in the 1930s. Why? We don't know!

Jesus' birth could so easily have been one of these skeletons in the closet. It involved a young, unwed mother, and a pregnancy and birth out of wedlock—all of which suggests impurity and shame. The surprise is that the Gospel writers bother to tell the story at all because it is a very risky story to tell.

The risk is that Jesus will be thought of not as an heir of an everlasting kingdom but as the bastard son of a peasant mother from a very small town. The risk is that the Gospel authors will be accused of wishful thinking—of sweeping an unpleasant anomaly in Jesus' biography under the carpet. The risk is that the Bible's explanation—that Jesus was "conceived by the Holy Spirit, born of the Virgin Mary"[41]—will seem far-fetched and inconceivable.

But I think the writers were well aware of this risk. And yet they told us the story, firstly, because they believed it was true (of course), but also secondly, because they believed that it told us what we need to know about Jesus—that he was born as a baby like any one of us, sharing the very stuff we are made out of, but also that he was from somewhere else. He was a new beginning: here was God intervening in the human story once and for all.

NOT ALL BEER AND SKITTLES

Jesus did not live a life that was all beer and skittles. He most certainly could have. At its best, human life can be quite a lark—especially in our times when we enjoy good health and advanced technology. But Jesus was born as a member of an oppressed people—a people whose homeland had been occupied for centuries. They were a people struggling to work out what their true identity was. In addition, it wasn't apparent that Jesus was destined for greatness: he was born into an obscure, fringy family living in the boondocks. He lived his life in primitive conditions in dwellings without flushing toilets and air-conditioning.

Furthermore, Jesus was tempted and tested by his life in the flesh just as we are. He was tested by the devil himself to give up worship of the true God, and to take the easy path to instant pleasure, safety and power (Luke 4:1-13). He was presented with opportunities to exploit his popularity and his powers to his own advantage. He was a charismatic young man who had a number of women among his followers, so no doubt he was tempted to use them for physical pleasure. He was tempted to flee from what he knew to be his real task—offering himself as a sacrifice for the sins of the people. At the very last moment, he pleaded with God, "Remove this cup from me" (Mark 14:35-36)!

It was hard. And yet he did not fail. I suppose you might be forgiven for feeling a certain scepticism at this point: surely the writers of the accounts of Jesus' life have glossed over a few of his imperfections here and there? To that suggestion, I would say this: it is actually very hard to write an account of a perfect, yet real, life. Whenever authors have tried to create a fictional character who is perfect, that character never seems real. Yet in the Gospels, Jesus comes across as real—compellingly real—and yet without the sin that scars the rest of us.

Why does this matter? It matters because here was human life as it ought to have been lived. Jesus is significant not only because of the way he avoided sin but also because of his remarkable acts of kindness and love. He was obedient to God in every sense—in the way that human beings were always supposed to be obedient to God the Father.

It matters, too, because it shows how evil human beings were in putting him to death. We crucified the best human being there has ever been. We happily disposed of our champion! We tore him apart. Even his friends ran away from him. His death is a sad sign of how low the rest of us have fallen.

And it matters because, finally, here was someone worthy—someone worthy enough to represent us in our business with God—someone worthy enough to pay the penalty for our sins because he had not fallen prey to sin's wiles.

Lastly, it matters because it tells us that we have a God who understands what it means to be tempted and tested. We have a God who is not distant from us—not unyielding in his harshness—but one who has been where we have to go. In the book of Hebrews, it's put like this: "For we do not have a high priest who is unable to sympathize with our weaknesses, but one who in every respect has been tempted as we are, yet without sin" (Heb 4:15).

TRUE HUMANISM

What really changed everything for Jesus' followers was the fact that he didn't stay dead. You get the sense that, during his life, they knew they were in the presence of someone great—certainly the greatest prophet and teacher of their time. They even recognized that he was God's chosen one, anointed for the task of saving his people. But I don't think that they really accounted for the surprise of seeing him again after he died. And that, as I say, seemed to change everything.

Their first reaction was fear—partly, I imagine, because seeing someone alive again who has just died is a very surprising thing. But I also think they reacted that way because they recognized that Jesus was not just a man, he was divine too. And when you meet God, the normal human reaction is to be very afraid.

They also realized pretty quickly that if Jesus was God, then he was someone they ought to worship. So Thomas, when he first saw him post-resurrection, said, "My Lord and my God!" (John 20:28)—and as well he might! This man was not just an incredible man but the Lord of all, the ruler of the universe.

Christians worship a human being—but not just any human being, of course. They worship a particular human being who showed himself worthy of being worshipped. The first Christians gave themselves to proclaiming exactly this—that Jesus is Lord, and therefore he is worthy to be worshipped and honoured as God. Christians ever since have been doing likewise.

This is why Christianity might better be known as 'humanism' because it is about the worship of the true human.

endnotes

1   Lewis Carroll, *Alice's Adventures in Wonderland and Through the Looking-Glass*, Penguin Classics, London, 1998 (1865 and 1872), pp. 40-1.

2   Michel Foucault, *The Order of Things*, Vintage, New York, 1994, p. 490.

3   United Nations, *Universal Declaration of Human Rights*, 1948, viewed 7 February 2007: http://www.un.org/Overview/rights.html

4   *Disclosure*, motion picture, Baltimore pictures, Washington, 1994. Distributed by Warner Bros, directed by Barry Levinson and starring Michael Douglas, Demi Moore and Donald Sutherland.

5   The Rolling Stones, 'I'm Free', *Out of Our Heads*, Decca Records, 1965. Music and lyrics by Mick Jagger and Keith Richards.

6   Australian Bureau of Statistics, 'Census of Population and Housing: Selected Social and Housing Characteristics, Australia', Canberra, Australia, 2003, viewed 7 February 2007: http://www.abs.gov.au/newmetadata4/2015.0_3.htm

7   Walter Truett Anderson, *Reality Isn't What It Used to Be: Theatrical Politics, Ready-to-Wear Religion, Global Myths, Primitive Chic, and Other Wonders of the Postmodern World*, Harper & Row, San Francisco, 1990, p. 7.

8   I think Hugh Mackay said this in a newspaper article.

9   Christian Wienberg, 'Goldfish in blenders cause outrage', *The Independent*, 14 February 2000, viewed 7 February 2007: http://www.independent.co.uk/news/europe/goldfish-in-blenders-cause-outrage-724729.html

10   Aristotle, *Politics*, Book III, chapter 6, trans. Benjamin Jowett, NuVision Publications, Sioux Falls, 2004.

11   *Alive*, motion picture, Film Andes S.A., 1993. Distributed by Touchstone Pictures and Paramount Pictures, Burbank and Hollywood, directed by Frank Marshall and starring Ethan Hawke, Vincent Spano and Josh Hamilton.

12   Buzz McClain, 'A real, live "Alive" survivor relates his Andes ordeal', viewed 8 February 2007: http://wesclark.com/rrr/alive2.html

13 CS Lewis, *Mere Christianity*, Harper Collins, New York, 2001 (1952), p. 98.

14 For those who have never heard this term, a 'muffin top' is that part of your flesh that spills out over the waistline of your trousers.

15 Anthony Giddens, *Modernity and Self-Identity: Self and Society in the Late Modern Age*, Polity Press, 1991, pp. 99-103.

16 Susan Holtham, 'Body Piercing in the West: a Sociological Inquiry', *Body Modification Ezine*, 23 November 1997, viewed 12 February 2008: http://www.bmezine.com/pierce/bodypier.html

17 This was the title of a Christian dieting book by Patricia Banta Kreml, first published in 1978 (Logos International, Plainfield).

18 Bloodhound Gang, 'The Bad Touch', *Hooray for Boobies*, Jimmy Franks Recording Company, Geffen Records, 1999. Music and lyrics by Jimmy Pop.

19 John Milton, 'Sonnet 19', *Poems, &c. upon Several Occasions*, London, 1673.

20 *Declaration of the Rights of Man and of the Citizen*, approved by the National Assembly of France, 26 August, 1789, viewed 12 February 2007: http://www.hrcr.org/docs/frenchdec.html

21 Dylan Thomas, 'Do not go gentle into that good night', *The Poems of Dylan Thomas*, New Directions, New York, 1971 (1952), p. 162.

22 The Smashing Pumpkins, 'Bullet with Butterfly Wings', *Mellon Collie and the Infinite Sadness*, Virgin Records, 1995. Music and lyrics by Billy Corgan.

23 Martin Luther, *Concerning Christian Liberty*, trans. RS Grignon, The Harvard Classics, vol. 36, PF Collier & Son, New York, 1910, p. 353. Viewed online 15 February 2008: http://www.ctsfw.edu/etext/luther/freedom/harvard/freedom2.txt

24 Eminem, 'Cleanin' Out My Closet', *The Eminem Show*, Aftermath/Interscope, New York, 2003. Music and lyrics by Eminem.

25 M Scott Peck, *People of the Lie*, Touchstone, New York, 1983, pp. 51-52.

26 Viewed 8 February 2008: http://en.wiktionary.org/wiki/honour

27 Luce Irigaray, *An Ethics of Sexual Difference*, trans. Carolyn Burke and Gillian C Gill, Cornell University Press, Ithaca, 1993, p. 3.

28 Martin Luther King Jr, 'I Have a Dream' speech, Washington DC, 28 August 1963.

29 Jimi Hendrix, 'Castles Made of Sand', *Axis: Bold as Love*, Track Records and Barclay Records, 1967. Music and lyrics by Jimi Hendrix.

30 Philip Larkin, 'This Be The Verse', *High Windows*, Faber and Faber, London, 1974.

31 'Angels "favourite funeral song"', *BBC News*, 10 March 2005, viewed online 18 February 2008: http://news.bbc.co.uk/1/hi/entertainment/music/4336113.stm

32 Mitchell Stephens, 'Jacques Derrida', *The New York Times Magazine*, 23 January 1994, p. 25.

33 Emily Dickinson, 'Because I could not stop for Death', no. 712, *The Complete Poems of Emily Dickinson*, ed. Thomas H. Johnson, Little, Brown and Company, London, 1961, p. 350.

34 William Shakespeare, *Hamlet*, III.I.56, ed. Philip Edwards, The New Cambridge Shakespeare, Cambridge University Press, Cambridge, 2003.

35 I got this image from Helen Garner ('At the Morgue' in *True Stories*, Text Publishing, 1996, pp. 145-153).

36 Epictetus, *The Discourses*, trans. George Long, Hayes Barton Press, Raleigh, 2005, p. 9.

37 Donna Jeanne Haraway, *Modest_witness@Second_Millennium.Femaleman©_Meets_Oncomouse™: Feminism and Technoscience*, Routledge, New York, 1997.

38 Red Hot Chili Peppers, 'Can't Stop', *By the Way*, Warner Bros, 2003. Music and lyrics by Anthony Kiedis, John Frusciante, Flea and Chad Smith.

39 *Gladiator*, motion picture, Dreamworks, Glendale, 2000. Distributed by Dreamworks and Universal Studios, Glendale and Hollywood, directed by Ridley Scott and starring Russell Crowe, Joaquin Phoenix and Connie Nielsen.

40 Karl Barth, *Church Dogmatics*, vol. IV, *The Doctrine of Reconciliation*, trans. GW Bromiley, eds. GW Bromiley and TF Torrance, Continuum International Publishing Group, London and New York, 1977, p. 29.

41 As the Apostles' Creed summarizes it.

matthiasmedia

Matthias Media is a ministry team of like-minded, evangelical Christians working together to achieve a particular goal, as summarized in our mission statement:

To serve our Lord Jesus Christ, and the growth of his gospel in the world, by producing and delivering high quality, Bible-based resources.

It was in 1988 that we first started pursuing this mission together, and in God's kindness we now have more than 250 different ministry resources being distributed all over the world. These resources range from Bible studies and books through to training courses and audio sermons.

To find out more about our large range of very useful products, and to access samples and free downloads, visit our website:

www.matthiasmedia.com.au

How to buy our resources

1. Direct from us over the internet:
   – in the US: www.matthiasmedia.com
   – in Australia and the rest of the world: www.matthiasmedia.com.au

2. Direct from us by phone:
   – in the US: 1 866 407 4530
   – in Australia: 1800 814 360 (Sydney: 9663 1478)
   – international: +61-2-9663-1478

3. Through a range of outlets in various parts of the world. Visit **www.matthiasmedia.com.au/international.php** for details about recommended retailers in your part of the world, including www.thegoodbook.co.uk in the United Kingdom.

4. Trade enquiries can be addressed to:
   – in the US: sales@matthiasmedia.com
   – in the UK: sales@ivpbooks.com
   – in Australia and the rest of the world: sales@matthiasmedia.com.au

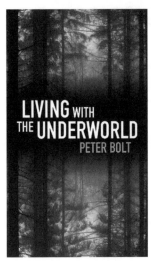